Rod Connell does it once again with his latest writing, "True Identity"...Rod's gift of wisdom and his writing style bring understanding to the biblical truth that others have so often complicated. As Rod tackles this subject of our true identity in Christ, he dispels the lies and confusion of the enemy of our souls, who tries his best to keep us locked up in mediocrity and complacency. "True Identity" brings clarity to the question often asked by many: why are we, the church, not more effective as new creatures in Christ? This book will be a life-changing book of freedom and fresh revelation for you. It will help you discover your own true identity, reach your God-given potential and become the person God created you to be.

—Daren Carstens, Pastor
Enjoy Church, Alton and O'Fallon IL

TRUE
IDENTITY

ROD CONNELL

TRUE IDENTITY

A Believer's Full Inheritance in Christ

TATE PUBLISHING
AND ENTERPRISES, LLC

True Identity
Copyright © 2016 by Rod Connell. All rights reserved.

No part of this publication may be reproduced, stored in a retrieval system or transmitted in any way by any means, electronic, mechanical, photocopy, recording or otherwise without the prior permission of the author except as provided by USA copyright law.

Scripture quotations marked (kjv) are taken from the *Holy Bible, King James Version*, Cambridge, 1769. Used by permission. All rights reserved.

Scripture quotations marked (nkjv) are taken from the *New King James Version*. Copyright © 1982 by Thomas Nelson, Inc. Used by permission. All rights reserved.

This book is designed to provide accurate and authoritative information with regard to the subject matter covered. This information is given with the understanding that neither the author nor Tate Publishing, LLC is engaged in rendering legal, professional advice. Since the details of your situation are fact dependent, you should additionally seek the services of a competent professional.

The opinions expressed by the author are not necessarily those of Tate Publishing, LLC.

Published by Tate Publishing & Enterprises, LLC
127 E. Trade Center Terrace | Mustang, Oklahoma 73064 USA
1.888.361.9473 | www.tatepublishing.com

Tate Publishing is committed to excellence in the publishing industry. The company reflects the philosophy established by the founders, based on Psalm 68:11,
"The Lord gave the word and great was the company of those who published it."

Book design copyright © 2016 by Tate Publishing, LLC. All rights reserved.
Cover design by Bill Francis Peralta
Interior design by Shieldon Alcasid

Published in the United States of America

ISBN: 978-1-68237-678-2
Religion / Christian Life / Spiritual Growth
15.11.05

Dedicated to the perfect One, Christ Jesus, the Son of the living God, who was willing to die for us, setting us free and making us heirs to His unsearchable riches; to our Father for His inexorable love and the grace to share His glory; and to the Holy Spirit, whose light and work have made it all real to darkened hearts and brought to fruition the eternal purpose of God.

"As many as are led by the Spirit of God, these are the sons of God. For you did not receive the spirit of bondage again to fear, but you have received the Spirit of adoption by whom we cry out, 'Abba, Father.' The Spirit Himself bears witness with our spirit that we are the children of God, and if children, then heirs—heirs of God and joint heirs with Christ, if indeed we suffer with Him, that we may also be glorified together."

—Romans 8:14–17

Full Inheritance

Your full inheritance, please claim,
Live as paupers no more!
All included in His great Name
Is yours, no longer poor…

Abundant now, eternal then,
Do not settle for less:
Will and testament both within,
Release them and be blessed!

Contents

Introduction 15

Part 1: Some Other Gospel 17

    Early Attempts at Distortions.............................. 19
    The Judaizers.. 23
    The Troubles in Corinth...................................... 27
    Christ Walking among the Churches.................. 35

        Ephesus: The Post-apostolic Church 36
        Smyrna: The Suffering Church 40
        Pergamos: The Compromising Church....... 42
        Thyatira: The Corrupted Church 44
        Sardis: The "Reformed" Church.................. 48
        Philadelphia: The Faithful Church.............. 49
        Laodicea: the Apostate Church 51

    A Quick Summary of the Seven Churches 55
    The Overcomers... 57
    Are All Believers Overcomers?............................ 67
    The Church in America Today............................ 73
    Easy Believism and the Prosperity Gospel 77
    Conclusion of Part 1 83

Part 2: Recovering the True Gospel 85

    Soul and Spirit 87
    Repentance 93
    Crucified with Christ 103
    A Mystery Revealed 107
    The Trigger of Life 111
    An Exchanged Life 113
    Resting in God 117
    Revivals 121
    Before Going On 125

Part 3: Living by the Indwelling Life 129

    Inheritance and Dominion 131
    A Beginning 139
    Living in Community 143
    Simplifying 149
    Communion 153
    Fruit That Lasts 157
    Builders of the Kingdom 161
    Glory 165
    Life and Death 169
    Summing Up 175

Afterword 181

Introduction

SINCE HIS DEFEAT by Christ on Calvary, Satan's most effective weapon of survival has been division—dividing the Body of Christ. He has utilized an assortment of schemes to accomplish that end and, thus far, has been quite successful. False teaching crept in almost immediately: in his epistles to various churches, we find the apostle Paul confronting the problem early on, striving to get believers back on track, refusing to follow any message other than the true gospel of Christ.

Unfortunately, Paul was unable to stop the bleeding; division proliferated, and today we find the church to be a confusing quagmire of schisms and conflicting beliefs. The end result? Weakness. Weakness by diminishing our true identity in Christ. Today mostly carnal weapons are being employed in the spiritual endeavors of the church, and the flesh is no match for Satan.

I have spent most of my Christian life in search of the true gospel of Christ. Being born into a country that believes in freedom of religion is certainly a good thing, but it can also be a hindrance. There are so many versions of our faith in Christ out there! For those born into Christian homes, most simply follow the doctrines of the denomination into which they are born, unaware of the changes from the original pattern that may have taken place. Others remain in the churches where they attend at the time of their salvation experience. Still others wander from church to church (most of what is called church growth is actually the result of migration of attendees and not new believers).

After my own conversion, as I was studying the book of Acts, I was struck by the great disparity between the first century church and the modern church. The differences are immense! While I understand that the birth and growth of the early church was unique and not necessarily something that should be seen as a perfect template for the operation of the church throughout the ages, some characteristics should have remained. The obvious question is: What happened?

How has the enemy of our souls become so successful at dividing and weakening the Body of Christ? The end result has been the fulfillment of 2 Timothy 3:5, "Having a form of godliness but denying its power." The purpose of this book is to uncover what has gone wrong and to find our way back to what is true, to separate the authentic from the counterfeit. We must recover and live who we truly are as disciples of Christ! For until we do, Satan will prolong his stay and retain his position as the prince of this world. It is time that we are no longer fooled by the lies and wiles of the devil, time for the manifestation of the sons and daughters of God; time for believers to come into their full inheritance in Christ.

PART 1

SOME OTHER GOSPEL

Early Attempts at Distortions

> "O foolish Galatians! Who has bewitched you that you should not obey the truth, before whose eyes Jesus Christ was clearly portrayed among you as crucified?…I marvel that you are turning away so soon from Him who called you in the grace of Christ to a different gospel, which is not another; but there are some who trouble you and want to pervert the gospel of Christ. But even if we, or an angel from heaven, preach any other gospel to you than what you have received, let him be accursed."
>
> —Galatians 3:1; 1:6–8

ALL SATANIC LIES and maneuvers since the death, resurrection, and ascension of the Lord Jesus Christ have been aimed at producing "some other gospel," any other gospel than the true gospel of Christ. For any other gospel is no gospel at all, impotent and useless, no matter how well-intentioned; products of the flesh, and flesh can never give birth to Spirit (John 3:6).

The first issue that arose was the dispute between Jews and Gentiles (non-Jews) when it came to the matter of salvation. Jews believed salvation was for them alone. They viewed Gentiles as unclean and held them in no more regard than dogs. Gentiles could convert to Judaism, but that was the only way they could ever find favor with God.

Therefore, when Peter was commanded by the Holy Spirit to go to the house of Cornelius (Acts 10), who was a Gentile, he struggled mightily with the order. It took the vision of the great sheet full of unclean animals with the command to "Rise, Peter. Kill and eat" (Acts 10:13) to appear three times for Peter to be convinced and agree. While Peter was still puzzling over the vision, three men who had been sent from Cornelius appeared to take Peter to Cornelius. I am sure that this further confused Peter, but then the Holy Spirit spoke, assuring him that he should indeed go with them, for it was He who had sent them.

For God had also spoken to Cornelius in a vision: an angel appeared and told Cornelius, "Now send men to Joppa, and send for Simon, whose surname is Peter" (Acts 10:5). The angel even explained exactly where Peter was staying, "with Simon, a tanner, whose house is by the sea" (10:6). So the Lord made emphatic connections with both men! Perhaps, this was necessary for both of them to be persuaded, for such a mission was indeed a strange one for both a Jew and a Gentile.

Cornelius had gathered his relatives and close friends for the meeting that was to take place. Once the two men told of their respective visions, Peter spoke and said, "In truth I perceive that God shows no partiality. But in every nation whoever fears Him and works righteousness is accepted by

Him…He is Lord of all" (Acts 10:34a; 36b). And while Peter was still preaching the Word of salvation to them, the Holy Spirit fell upon all the Gentiles present, even as it had on the disciples on the Day of Pentecost. "Those of the circumcision who believed were astonished," Acts 10:45 declares.

With all the substantiations from the Spirit that what had occurred was indeed of God, Peter answered and said, "Can anyone forbid water, that these should not be baptized who have received the Holy Spirit just as we have" (Acts 10:47)? All the Gentiles were then baptized in water, and Peter stayed with them a few days (undoubtedly to rejoice and to instruct them in the basics of their new faith and life in Christ).

Of course, this was not the end of it. When Peter came up to Jerusalem, he was questioned as to why he would do such a forbidden thing. He gave an account of all that had happened and ended his discourse with these words, "And as I began to speak, the Holy Spirit fell upon them, as upon us at the beginning…If therefore, God gave them the same gift as He gave us when we believed on the Lord Jesus Christ, who was I that I could withstand God" (Acts 11:15, 17)? This ended the argument; all those present perceived that salvation had indeed been extended to all men and was not confined to the Jews. This was a tremendous revelation! Some other gospel had been nipped in the bud, and the Holy Spirit responded by a tremendous influx of new believers, with Paul and Barnabas preaching the Word for a whole year in Antioch to all who would hear it, both Jews and Gentiles.

The Judaizers

THE JUDAIZERS SEEM to have been a group of Jewish Christians in the first century CE who preached to the recently founded churches of the Gentiles the need to conform to the Law of Moses, even after the death and resurrection of Jesus Christ. The group originated in Jerusalem; we know little about them, only that, at least, some were likely Pharisees (Acts 15:5). We do not know how organized they were or any names of any individuals within the movement. But this we do know: they *attempted to make Jews out of Gentile Christians.* Emphasis mine. (astudyofdenominations.com/history/Judaizers)

The conflict between the two faiths, Judaism and Christianity, continued for some time. For although many Jews realized that Gentiles were also to be included through faith in Christ, a certain group arose who taught that they must also keep the Law of Moses; in other words, they had to become Jews in order to become Christians! Again, "some other gospel"…faith plus works.

Acts 15 gives a detailed account of this debate. The chapter opens with these words: "And certain men came down from Judea and taught the brethren, 'Unless you are circumcised according to the custom of Moses, you cannot be saved'" (15:1). So Paul and Barnabas and certain others went to Jerusalem, to the apostles and elders, to discuss this question. On their way to Jerusalem, Paul and Barnabas passed through Phoenicia and Samaria preaching the Word, and many Gentiles came to faith in Christ. When the two apostles reached Jerusalem, they reported all God had done along the way.

But, of course, many Pharisees were unconvinced and repeated their demand for all to keep the Law of Moses, whether Jew or Gentile. All the apostles and leaders then came together to discuss the matter. After much dispute, Peter rose up and repeated his experience in the house of Cornelius as proof that one did not have to keep the law and customs of Moses in order to be saved. James, the leader of the council, then spoke and reminded them of Amos 9:11 and 12, in which the prophet foretold that the Messiah would restore the tabernacle of David and a time when all might be saved, even the Gentiles.

The Pharisees, supposedly experts in the scriptures, should have also known the words of Isaiah: "Indeed He says, 'It is too small a thing You should be my Servant to raise up the tribes of Jacob, and to restore the preserved ones of Israel; I will also give You as a light to the Gentiles, that You should be my salvation to the ends of the earth'" (Isaiah 49:6).

James then made an interesting decision (agreed to by all who were present): not to trouble Gentile believers on issues like circumcision and other matters of the law…but with four exceptions: "to abstain from things polluted by idols, from sexual immorality, from things strangled, and from blood" (Acts 15:20). A most curious decision, don't you think? Of course, the decision did not mean that these stipulations were required to be saved but that they should be observed *after* salvation.

I am not exactly certain why these concessions were made. Certainly, any form of sexual immorality should be avoided by all born-again believers. And it must be remembered that most of the Gentiles had been idol worshipers before becoming Christians, so any practice that might have drawn them back to some form of idolatry had to be avoided. Perhaps, the decision helped appease the Judaizers. But what must be remembered is that the decision was not only the conclusion of men but also God, for the letter sent to Gentile believers in Antioch, Syria, and Cilicia declares, "For it seemed good to the Holy Spirit, and to us, to lay upon you no greater burden than these necessary things" (Acts 15:28).

Note: Later on, we find the apostle Paul saying that idols are really nothing and that he would eat meat sacrificed to idols *unless* it offended a weaker brother, in which case, for the sake of the other, he would abstain. Also, many Jews objected to Timothy entering the temple because he was only half-Jewish by blood and, therefore, not a true Jew, so Paul had Timothy circumcised to circumvent the objections. Such compromises seem to fall under what Paul calls in 1 Corinthians 9:22 being "all things to all men" that he might save some. The whole passage reads like this:

> For although I am free from all men, I have made myself a servant of all, that I might win the more; and to the Jews I became as a Jew, that I might win Jews; to those who are under the law, as under the law, that I might win those who are under the law; to those who are without law, as without law (not being without law toward God, but under law toward Christ), that I might win those who are without law; to the weak I became as weak, that I might win the weak. I have become all things to men, that I might by all means save some. (1 Corinthians 9:19–22)

So Paul was willing to compromise on nonessentials, things that made no difference one way or the other, and it is obvious that the Holy Spirit agreed and honored this approach. The book of Romans continues to address the Jewish/Gentile situation: chapter 9 declares that God's mercy is on whomever He chooses; chapter 10 affirms that salvation is open to all; chapter 11 depicts God grafting Jews and Gentiles into one tree; and in chapter 14, Paul goes into great detail about living together in love and unity, not allowing anything to divide— the chapter heading in the NKJV (New King James Version) is "The Law of Liberty and the Law of Love."

But returning to the council at Jerusalem, the most important outcome to keep in mind is that once again, "some other gospel" was averted (at least, for the time-being).

The Troubles in Corinth

> "Now I plead with you, brethren, by the name of our Lord Jesus Christ, that you all speak the same thing, and that there be no divisions among you, but that you be perfectly joined together in the same mind and in the same judgment."
>
> —1 Corinthians 1:10

The church at Corinth was fraught with issues and practices that threatened to tear the church apart. The central problem? Division. Paul had received word from believers in the house of Chloe that there were "contentions" (1:11) among them. So after greeting the believers with much praise for their knowledge and spiritual gifts, Paul immediately began to confront them with their departures from the truth of the gospel.

The formation of non-biblical factions was the first problem Paul addressed. Of course, the difficulty here is that factions can become sects, even cults, if left unattended. It seems that the believers at Corinth were separating themselves on the basis of who their favorite teacher was or who had been instrumental in their conversion experience.

Some said they were "of Paul," others "of Apollos" or "of Cephas." Still others claimed to be "of Christ," probably to declare that they were not among those who were quibbling over such labels!

(How we still love to give names to things! Think of all the names churches have chosen for themselves. By so doing, they seek to distinguish how they are different from other churches right down the street. This practice does not unite; it divides! Then there are those who call themselves nondenominational or interdenominational; still others use the term "full Gospel"—does that mean all others are only partial gospel churches?)

Paul did his best to dispel such divisions by asking, "Is Christ divided" (1:13)? The implication is that all believers are of Christ and Christ alone; there can be no other distinctions. In Revelation 2 and 3, the seven churches Christ mentions are all addressed as "*the* church" at Ephesus, Smyrna, Pergamos, etc. Singular, church not churches, the only difference being the location of each. For that is how Christ sees the church; all other names and distinctions are man-made and the products of division.

In chapter 2, Paul seems to be addressing the problem of spiritual pride, which is certainly instrumental in the creation of division. Paul stresses the importance of humility, especially in spiritual matters; that all true wisdom comes from God and, therefore, is nothing by which to become puffed up. Next, the apostle points out the difference between spiritual wisdom and man-made wisdom—one the product of the Holy Spirit, the other a creation of the flesh. True spiritual wisdom never leads to division; all division comes from the wisdom of man, an intrusion of the flesh into spiritual affairs.

Spiritual immaturity becomes the next issue Paul chooses to discuss. For although the believers were commended for their knowledge and spiritual gifts (1 Corinthians 1:4–8), they were yet "carnal" in other ways. I believe this indicates that in the battle between flesh and Spirit, the flesh was triumphing in certain areas—areas that, maturing in Christ, should have already overcome. This should be a warning to us today: just because we are teaching the right things and the gifts of the Spirit are operating well does not equate itself to maturity. So many covet spiritual gifts (which we are indeed advised to do, 1 Corinthians 12:31), but we must not mistake the operation of the gifts as proof of maturity in Christ. After all, gifts are free! And the church at Corinth should cause us to question such a conclusion.

Chapter 3 again brings up the issue of factions on the basis of favorite teachers or ministers of the Gospel (Paul had already mentioned this in chapter 1). He explains that each in the Body of Christ has a part to play (some plant, others water the new growth, but it is God who gives the increase, not the work of any man). He compares such practices and preferences to building on some other foundation than Christ, who is the only true foundation in the eyes of God (again, "some other gospel" was intruding on the true gospel of Christ).

Paul also reminds them that their body is the temple of the Holy Spirit; that the blessed third member of the Trinity dwells within them and that they should, therefore, be very careful not to defile their body. Paul does not elaborate on exactly what the Corinthian believers were doing to defile their bodies, but his warning was sharp: "If anyone defiles the temple of God, God will destroy him. For the temple of God is holy, which temple you are" (3:17).

Sexual immorality becomes the next subject Paul addresses: it seems that a man in the congregation had taken up with his father's wife (his own stepmother?), and the church had tolerated it. Paul's condemnation of such a vile thing was swift and harsh: "In the name of our Lord Jesus Christ, when you are gathered together, along with my spirit, with the power of our Lord Jesus Christ, deliver such a one to Satan for the destruction of the flesh, that his spirit may be saved in the day of the Lord Jesus" (1 Corinthians 5:4–5). The man was to be expelled from the church so that he might come to himself and repent (which he actually did do, for this is alluded to in Paul's second letter to the Corinthians, chapter 2, verses 5 to 8). Paul admonishes them to receive the man back into the congregation with love and forgiveness, which is what we always must do when a brother or sister has sinned but then truly repents.

The apostle then takes up the case of believers suing other believers in a court of law rather than settling the matter "in house," so to speak. Better yet, he says, why not just be wronged and let the matter go, committing it to God? Paul next reminds them not to behave like worldly people with a long list of sins to avoid: fornication, idolatry, adultery, homosexuality, sodomy, thievery, coveting, alcoholism, reviling, extortion! Does that indicate that there were actually those in the church at Corinth who were guilty of such transgressions? Or just a warning that those who practice such things will not inherit the kingdom of God (6:10)? In verse 11, he reminds them they were once like this but were then washed, sanctified, and justified, therefore, freed from such sinning.

Sexual impropriety again surfaces and is condemned (6:13–15), so apparently this was still a problem among some believers at Corinth (otherwise, why would Paul have mentioned it again?). He repeats his reminder that their bodies are the temple of the Holy Spirit, and, therefore, should not be used to commit sexual sins; that as members of the Body of Christ, joining their bodies to a harlot was like joining Christ to her! Chapter 6 concludes with the words, "Therefore glorify God *in your body* and in your spirit, which are God's" (verse 20), emphasis mine.

The principles of marriage from God's perspective consume all of chapter 7, covering cases of believers yoked to unbelievers, as well as whether or not those in Christ should marry at all. Paul says he would prefer that all were as him, whether single or widows, to remain unmarried, enabling them to give more time to the Lord and His work. But knowing that some were unable to "exercise self-control" (7:9), they should marry, which is "better than to burn with passion" (8:9). Verse 24 summarizes Paul's view on the subject: "Brethren, let each one remain with God in that state in which he was called." If single, to remain single; if married, to remain married.

Much had gone awry in Corinth: from chapter 8 to chapter 16, Paul covered a number of other key issues: the need to be sensitive to conscience, especially in matters of eating and offending weaker brethren; the need of serving all men; doing all things for the sake of God's glory; gross violations of the Lord's Supper; the call to spiritual unity of believers; the proper use of spiritual gifts; a reminder of both the Lord's resurrection and their own. Paul closed with some final instructions, personal plans, and greetings.

All the foregoing were serious departures from the true gospel of Christ and, if allowed to go unchecked, threatened the very witness of the church at Corinth. Greater weakness and division would be the inevitable result. Paul was quite harsh in his assessment of the situation, but he had to be if he hoped to correct it. In his second letter to the Corinthians, he was much more conciliatory and kind, perhaps, because his first letter had made a difference. A true minister must say it like it is, for that is both his call and obligation; for if he does not, he will be held accountable to the Lord (Ezekiel 3:18–19).

Christ Walking among the Churches

"Some other gospel" has continued to be the aim of satanic strategy for weakening the Body of Christ throughout church history. This can be clearly seen in Paul's epistles to the other churches and to certain individuals (Timothy, Titus, and Philemon) as well as the epistles of James, Peter, John, and Jude. In the book of Revelation chapters 2 and 3, when Christ surveyed and assessed the spiritual conditions of the seven churches, deviations from the true gospel were quite obvious. These were certainly actual churches in Asia Minor at the time the apostle received his revelation during his exile on the island of Patmos. But many biblical scholars have also seen the seven churches as representatives of the entire church age, the periods through which the church as a whole has passed. Let us take this point of view and examine what Christ had to say about each church.

Ephesus: The Post-apostolic Church

*Ephesus: Biblical meaning is *desirable*.

The revelation of Christ to the apostle John begins with the church at Ephesus. The Lord's assessment of the spiritual condition there was initially quite positive: the believers at Ephesus were praised for their work, labor, and patience and their discernment of false apostles and hating evil (chapter 2, verses 2 and 3). But then in verse 4, Christ pinpoints their failure: they had "left their first love." After all the commendable things they had been doing, this one fault surely wasn't all that serious…or was it?

Verse 5 informs us that it is extremely important, so critical that Christ says, "Remember therefore from where you have fallen; repent and do the first works, or else I will come to you quickly and remove your lampstand from its place—unless you repent." There is much to consider here, lest we make the same mistake, so let's pause and think about it.

First love and first works are linked, which seems to say that their first works as believers were purely motivated by their first love of Christ but that this had changed. The works had continued, but the first love had been left behind. What had gone wrong? What is the nature of this *first* love Jesus is talking about?

Think of your own experience…what was one of your greatest desires after the moment of salvation and the realization of how much the Lord loves us? Was it not to share that love so that others might experience it as well? No ulterior motives, no thought about personal gain, simply allowing the love of Christ within to be released and bless others.

But how does one preserve that kind of love, and what are the forces that can work against it? Certainly, our ancient foe, the devil, has much to do with it, as does the frailty of our own flesh. The enemy of our souls works overtime once we come to Christ: the last thing he wants is for any of us to become fully mature in Christ, for that would threaten his very existence as the prince of this world. At the same time, the Holy Spirit is in the maturing business, which at times requires Him to allow trials and tribulations to come our way as the means to our growth. Christ Himself warned us that in this world, we *will* have tribulations (John 16:33); but then He goes on to say, "But be of good cheer, I have overcome the world."

But in spite of His reassurance, our flesh often grows weary, and we don't always understand why we are under such attacks and discouragements; in short, it becomes so easy to "cool off" in our passion for Christ. We continue to do the work, but that first love wanes. This is the experience of almost all believers, even the most committed; there is no way to avoid it. So what are we to do to remedy such a condition?

First of all, we must realize it and repent! Jesus says it twice (chapter 2, verse 5). And in our prayer of repentance, we can implore the Lord to rekindle our love for Him. But the key is the life of Christ that indwells us: why else would He tell us to be of good cheer and promise peace in the midst of trials? What benefit to us is it that *He* has overcome the world if we cannot access that victory?

The good news is that we can! Continually surrendering our will to His will releases the power of His Life to come forth and prevail! Some have called this an exchanged life, ours for His; others disagree and stop short of calling the dynamics of that transaction an exchanged life. But whatever one calls it, it works and is the very way we are to live once we come to Christ. Paul reminded the believers at Corinth (and us) that once we come to Christ, we are no longer "our own," that we were "bought at a price," even the life and precious blood of Christ (1 Corinthians 6:19–20). Paul also says in Galatians 2:20, "I have been crucified with Christ; it is no longer I who live, but Christ lives in me…"

With His life comes all of His virtues and victory, peace, and being of good cheer during trying times. By surrendering to His will, even as He did to His Father's, all that is His is ours! Any other approach is of the flesh and doomed to failure. Our first love will, of course, change as we mature in the Lord but that love should only deepen as we grow, and the works that follow will still be motivated by that love. I love the verse that says, "For the love of

Christ constrains us" (2 Corinthians 5:14, KJV; "compels us," NKJV). Our mutual love, His for us and ours for Him, will eventually constrain or compel us to only desire His will, and surrendering to that love is the answer to all problems…hallelujah!

Before we move to the church at Smyrna, we need to pause and consider a bit more the seriousness of leaving our first love. For after the church passed through a period of suffering (Smyrna), more serious problems and breaches of the true gospel began to surface: false teaching crept in at Pergamos, and by the time we reach Thyatira, the church had become a huge organization controlled by a false prophetess named Jezebel, guilty of teaching and seducing the Lord's servants with sexual immorality and idolatry.

Does such a progression of degradation indicate that this is the direct result of not repenting the leaving their first love at Ephesus?

And furthermore, if that is the case, how did it happen? To answer that question, we must remember that Satan and the flesh are given an opening if that first love is not regained. For it is the work of Satan and the flesh that causes one to leave their first love, and once this twosome enters the picture and is allowed to stay, "some other gospel" is the inevitable consequence. That is why we are to "walk by the Spirit" (Galatians 5:16–17) and not fulfill the lusts of the flesh, refusing to fall to the temptations or trials of the devil. The conquering life of the Lord that indwells us is always available to resist both the pull of the flesh and the wiles of Satan. All we need to do to access it is to stay in submission to His will in all things, even as He lived out His earthly life (in submission to the Father); this was His source of power over the flesh and the enemy, and it must be ours as well.

As a final point to remember, know that love for the Lord and others should come ahead of both works and correct doctrine. Rightly dividing the Word is essential to prevent being swayed by false teaching, but the importance of love outweighs even that (1 Corinthians 13), for divine love never divides.

Smyrna: The Suffering Church

Smyrna: Biblical meaning is *bitter, strong*.

Although he has not totally abandoned the use of persecution as a means to destroy the church, Satan learned early on that, for the most part, persecution has only resulted in growth, not destruction; an increase both in terms of numbers and depth of faith. Perhaps, it was at Smyrna that he first observed this interesting phenomenon. For the Lord warned the believers at Smyrna that a period of extreme persecution was about to begin: "Do not fear any of those things which you are about to suffer. Indeed, the devil is about to throw some of you into prison, that you may be tested, and you will have tribulation ten days.

Be faithful unto death, and I will give you the crown of life" (Revelation 2:10).

The Lord had already commended the church for its faithfulness: good works, graceful endurance of tribulations and physical poverty (although spiritually Christ calls them rich). He was also aware of the blasphemy of the false brethren in their midst, but their need for faithfulness was about to be increased: they were about to be severely tested, a period of time in which the enemy would be doing all he could to destroy them. But those same trials were going to be used by the Lord to refine them. This should remind us that anything the Lord allows to come into our life, especially trials and tribulations, are for our good and His glory (and often the good of others).

To drive this point home, remember those times in your own life: if you endured in faith, did you not come out closer to the Lord at the other end? Genesis 50:19–21 certainly stresses this truth. Joseph, who had gone through so many trials and years of suffering, spoke these words to his brothers (who were certain he would take revenge upon them for their parts in his pain): "Joseph said to them, 'Do not be afraid, for am I in the place of God? But as for you, you meant evil against me, but God meant it for good, in order to bring it about as it is this day, to save many people alive. Now therefore, do not be afraid; I will provide for you and your little ones.' And he comforted them and spoke kindly to them."

As to the number of days in which the believers at Smyrna would be allowed to suffer persecution and imprisonment—ten—we must consider the significance of that number. Although in other passages of scripture ten relates to human government and law, I don't believe that is its meaning here. Ten is also a number of a complete cycle, as in our decimal system: one system ends, and another begins every ten units. So I think the Lord was indicating that after a complete cycle (not a literal ten days), their suffering would come to an end; in other words, there would be an end in sight. Again, this is something we should always keep in mind during our times of trials and testing: they will be limited in duration; therefore, there is an encouragement to hang on in faith.

Smyrna was indeed about to experience very bitter times, but the Lord encouraged them to be strong, even unto death. Bitter and strong, the very meaning of the word *Smyrna* (an interesting connection, don't you think?).

Pergamos: The Compromising Church

Pergamos: Biblical meaning is *height, elevation*.

It is interesting to note that Christ did not mention any faults concerning the spiritual conditions at the church of Smyrna. Does this mean that there were none? I do not think so. I believe that the Lord had mercy on the believers at Smyrna because of the extreme suffering they were about to endure. He did not wish to lay any more upon them than that. But once we reach the church at Pergamos, we find that much had gone awry, that "some other gospel" was indeed taking root and gaining greater strength.

After praising them for their good works and holding fast to His name, not denying Him even when persecution had come, taking the life of Antipas (Christ calls him His "faithful martyr," verse 2:13), Christ makes mention of the place where they live as being "Satan's throne" (also verse 13). By this, I take it to mean that Pergamos was a site of great spiritual darkness, Satan's throne indicating the height or elevation to which the ways of the enemy had risen. That can be seen by what is mentioned next: false teaching had made deep inroads: "But I have a few things against you, because you have there those who hold the doctrine of Balaam, who taught Balak to put a stumbling block before the children of Israel, to eat things sacrificed to idols, and to commit sexual immorality. Thus you also have those who hold the doctrine of the Nicolaitans, which thing I hate" (2:14–15).

The story of Balaam and Balak can be found in Numbers 22–24, but the doctrine of the Nicolaitans is not so easy to track down. Rather than speculating on the possible source and teachings of this group, we should be satisfied to know that it is "some other gospel" and that the Lord hates it. At Ephesus, this doctrine had not been tolerated, but at Pergamos, it had been accepted by some of the believers.

That is why I label Pergamos the compromising church. For some other gospel to enter and contaminate, it requires both deception and compromise. Both of these dynamics were at work in Pergamos. Due to the conflict between the faithful and those who had been deceived and had compromised, division, of course, would also have raised its ugly head.

There was once again only one remedy: repent! I plan to write much more on repentance in a later section, the essential part it has to play, especially during periods of decline, and the need for revival and reform. Since we find ourselves in the present-day church at just such a juncture, it is imperative that we understand the critical role of repentance.

Thyatira: The Corrupted Church

Thyatira: Biblical meaning is "hill graveyard."

Like the other six churches in Revelation 2 and 3, there was much to commend in the church of Thyatira: Christ says these words of praise in 2:19: "I know your works, love, service, faith, and your patience; and as for your works, the last are more than the first." Quite a list of virtues and accomplishments! But what followed was scathing in its severity and scope:

> Nevertheless I have a few things against you, because you allow that woman Jezebel, who calls herself a prophetess, to teach and seduce my servants to

> commit sexual immorality and eat things sacrificed to idols. And I gave her time to repent of her sexual immorality, and she did not repent. Indeed I will cast her into a sickbed, and those who commit adultery with her into great tribulation, unless they repent of their deeds. I will kill her children with death, and all the churches shall know that I am He who searches the minds and hearts. And I will give to each one of you according to your works. (2:20–23)

A false prophetess had infiltrated the church *and was tolerated*…allowed to both teach and seduce the believers, enticing them to commit some form of sexual immorality and to eat food defiled by idol worship. How things had sunk that low is difficult to understand. Perhaps, some "spiritual" meaning was falsely attached to the deviant sexual practices (there had been temple prostitutes in their former "religious" rituals). And remember, the council at Jerusalem had forbidden the eating of foods sacrificed to idols. It, therefore, seems certain that the two transgressions were indeed leading some at Thyatira back to the idolatry they were to have left behind for good.

Another form of false teaching was also a major problem at Thyatira. While all believers did not adhere to it, some followed a form of satanic doctrine, probably disguised as hyper-spiritual. During the second and third century, when Christianity was in its infancy in the Western world, magicians and soothsayers roamed the countryside, teaching that only a select few were allowed to know the "deeper meaning" of the gospel—including them, of course. This aberration of the true gospel went by the name *gnosticism*, meaning knowledge. This may well be what Christ was referring to in Revelation 2:24…again, "some other gospel"!

Notice that the Lord had given Jezebel time to repent. He always grants time for repentance before judgment strikes; His love, mercy, and long suffering always precede the enactment of His justice. Jezebel had been given the time but had refused to change her ways, so the Lord was about to "cast her into a sickbed…kill her children with death" (Revelation 2:22, 23). Exactly how this judgment would be executed is difficult to discern (is Christ speaking figuratively or literally, spiritually, or physically?). Whatever the correct interpretation, the consequences were drastic!

Also note that the followers of this false gospel still had the opportunity to repent, as indicated by the word *unless* in verse 22. The charismatic leaders of cults always lead many astray (for this indeed sounds like the beginnings of a cult in Thyatira). If those who adhered to the false doctrines of Jezebel did not repent, however, their judgment would come as well in the form of "great tribulation" (verse 2:22). An interesting choice of words (perhaps, what is suggested is immediate trials for those at Thyatira who did not repent *and* passing through the great tribulation during end-times for all those still guilty of the same sins *then*).

Thankfully, there were still many in Thyatira who did not follow the spiritual harlotries of Jezebel. There has always been a faithful remnant in every age of the church that remain true to the gospel of Christ. To those in the Thyatiran church (and to the faithful today), Christ says, "Hold fast to what you have till I come" (2:25).

Many biblical scholars have noticed the similarity of the female figure mentioned in the church of Thyatira and the scarlet woman of Revelation 17 and 18, who is also called "Mystery, Babylon the great, the mother of harlots and of the abomination of the earth" (Revelation 17:5). Of course, in Revelation 17 and 18, the Great Tribulation is well underway, and the "woman" seems to be a false system of worship and corrupter of the nations. Did the departure from the true gospel in Thyatira give rise to such wicked practice? No one knows for sure, but the connection seems possible and is worth mentioning.

So what we have seen thus far is this: leaving the first love of Christ behind in Ephesus, suffering for the true gospel in Smyrna, compromising of the gospel in Pergamos, and deep spiritual corruption in Thyatira. What is it that we will find at our next stop in Sardis?

Note: Satan's *height* and *elevation* in Pergamos is a *hill* in Thyatira, but on the hill is a *graveyard*, very reminiscent of Christ's description of the scribes and Pharisees in Matthew 23:27–28: "Woe to you, scribes and Pharisees, hypocrites! For you are like whitewashed tombs which indeed appear beautiful outwardly, but inside are full of dead men's bones and all uncleanness." Many are the religious creations of man that fit this description, including, at least, a portion of the believers in Thyatira.

Sardis: The "Reformed" Church

Sardis: Biblical meaning is "prince of joy."

The church at Sardis is very interesting to consider. The Lord mentions their works but does not say what they were; instead, He comes straight to the point: they have a name or reputation of being spiritually alive but are actually dead. Christ goes on to command them to strengthen the things that remain (good things, I take it), for they too are about to die, and He has not found them perfect before God (chapter 3, verse 2). To avoid their death, they are to be watchful, remember how they have received and heard, and repent.

If indeed the church at Sardis had anything to do with the Reformation, they were not very highly commended by the Lord for the changes that took place. Certainly, the wretched condition of the church at Thyatira was in need of repentance and reform, but reading even a brief synopsis of the Reformation reveals division among the reformers themselves: each emphasized different changes that needed to be made. So as a result, the movement was splintered into yet further divisions and factions!

Certainly, this was far from "perfect before God."

Again, mercifully, the Lord was giving the believers at Sardis time to repent. And there was a remnant there who had not "defiled their garments" (3:4), but what had begun as a real need had ended, as only a faint shadow of what the Lord had wanted to see happen. Parts of the true gospel had been recovered at Sardis (front and center, salvation by faith alone and not a combination of faith and works), but much remained the same, needing more attention and correction for more life to return. And division proliferated: what God had meant unto good for reformation, the enemy had used to further weaken the church. The true gospel had been diluted and reduced again to "some other gospel," to the point of near impotence.

Philadelphia: The Faithful Church

Philadelphia: Biblical meaning is "loving people."

The church at Philadelphia, in many ways, was (and is) the ideal church. No faults were mentioned, only praise.

> I know your works. See, I have set before you an open door, and no one can shut it; for you have a little strength, have kept My word, and have not denied My name. Indeed I will make those of the synagogue of Satan, who say they are Jews and are not, but lie—indeed I will make them come and worship before your feet, and to know that I have

loved you. Because you have kept My command to persevere, I will also keep you from the hour of trial which shall come upon the whole world, to test those who dwell in the earth. (Revelation 3:8–10)

Certainly, this was Christ's assessment of the church at Philadelphia during John's exile on Patmos. But is it not much more than that? Is it not the pattern for faithfulness throughout the ages? Watchman Nee called the church at Philadelphia "the faithful little flock." Is this not a good description of how the church should always conduct itself in a fallen and broken world? The church at Philadelphia seems to have been small in number and only having a "little strength"…but they had been faithful to keep His Word, not denying His name and obeying His command to persevere (in spite of being surrounded by false brethren, which Christ called "those of the synagogue of Satan"). Is this not all, in brief, we are called upon to do today? Thank the Lord that there have always been just such faithful remnants of believers throughout the church age! Without them, Satan would have been completely successful at subverting the true gospel of Christ. The faithful remnants have always passed the true gospel down to the next generation, ensuring its survival.

Such faithfulness at Philadelphia was so honored by the Lord that He set an "open door" before them that nothing could shut! They were free to enter and receive all the blessings of God and to exit to take blessings to others.

And Christ promised to keep them from the "hour of trial" that would come upon the whole world to test those on the earth. Surely, this is a reference to the Great Tribulation and the requirements of God to escape it. For those who truly live in the way described at Philadelphia will have no need to be tested, for they will have already been tested and passed! That is why it is so critical to be a "wise virgin" now (Matthew 25), willing to submit to Christ no matter what: by doing that, we will keep His Word and not deny His name, will keep His command to persevere, and will recognize and resist any attempt to pervert the true gospel of Christ.

If we are living in the manner just described, like the believers at Philadelphia, Christ's Word to *us* is also to "hold fast what you have, that no one may take your crown" (Revelation 3:11). Hallelujah and maranatha! Even so, come quickly, Lord Jesus!

Laodicea: the Apostate Church

Laodicea: Biblical meaning is "opinion or decision of the people."

We have come full circle and arrived at what many believe is the condition of the modern-day church: lukewarm with little or no spiritual life (but completely unaware of it), exhibiting a form of godliness but lacking the power of the true gospel. Here is what Christ had to say to Laodicean believers and to us as well (if we are suffering from the same condition):

> I know your works, that you are neither cold nor hot. I could wish you were cold or hot. So then, because you are lukewarm, and neither cold nor hot, I will vomit you out of My mouth. Because you say, 'I am rich, have become wealthy, and have need of nothing'—and do not know that you are wretched, poor, blind, and naked—I counsel you to buy from Me gold refined in the fire, that you may be rich; and white garments, that you may be clothed, that the shame of your nakedness may not be revealed; and anoint your eyes with eye salve, that you may see. (Revelation 3:15–18)

Wretched! That is the one word that best describes the believers at Laodicea, and not knowing it compounded the situation and the Lord's indictment. Like in the American church today, the Laodicean church seems to have been greatly blessed materially, so much so that it had put them to sleep to their true condition and need. Spiritually, they were in poverty, pacifying themselves with the material blessings of God (probably thinking of this as proof of their spiritual maturity). It seems to be a flaw of human nature to forget the source of blessings once all physical needs are met, especially when those blessings are increased from needs to luxuries. Israel displayed this propensity many times in their history, eventually going into exile when the judgment of God fell. I pray that we in this country wake up before a similar judgment falls upon us!

"Gold refined in the fire"; to "buy" it from Him is the Lord's counsel. Gold represents the attributes of the divine nature, which we as believers are to partake of (2 Peter 1:4). But such precious gold is very costly; it must be refined in the fire, which means going through the harsh heat of trials and passing through to the other side by submitting to the will of Christ. For the setting of self-will aside in favor of the will of God, this is the "price" that must be paid.

One who fails to do this is "naked" before God, unable to hide their lack of "white garments" and the fine linen of the true saints. But before such believers could even repent and follow the Lord's counsel, they had to be able to "see" their real condition, thus, the need of the eye salve of the Holy Spirit to heal their blindness by revelation. And their renewed spiritual sight had to be followed by deep repentance and zeal to turn and go the other way, following the Lord wherever He might lead.

Are we today most like the Laodicean church? If so, and I think many of us are, the counsel given to the Laodiceans is the same counsel the Lord gives to us…how will we respond while there is yet time?

A Quick Summary of the Seven Churches

A STUDY OF church history does seem to indicate that the church has passed through all seven stages of the churches of Revelation 2 and 3. It is not that one stage ended and the next began, each stage neatly and completely exhibited before the beginning of the next; rather, some characteristics of all seven churches have existed throughout and yet exist today. But each stage has had its salient characteristic, which is what I have tried to emphasize in my discussion of the seven churches. Obviously, we have been given this portion of scripture to warn us and to prevent us from making the same mistakes.

It is my contention that all the deceit and distortions of the enemy throughout the church age have been aimed at one goal: the creation of "some other gospel" spawned by false teaching and division. For as Paul said, any other gospel is no gospel at all. In the process of emasculating and changing the true gospel, the Body of Christ has been made weak and robbed of its glorious, true identity and full inheritance in Christ. It is past time for us to repent, repent, repent! Repent and regain the position of who we truly are in Christ, for this is the only way we can "hasten His coming" (2 Peter 3:12) and not lose ground to the enemy.

The Overcomers

As stated before, there have always been faithful remnants of the true gospel throughout church history. Many have paid with their lives for not compromising their commitment to the Lord, and even today, in diverse places in the world, the same kind of persecution is rampant. We must never forget to pray for our brothers and sisters in the Lord who are in constant danger for their belief in Christ. Pray for relief from their suffering and also for strength to remain overcomers.

Revelation 2 and 3 call these faithful remnants overcomers, and they are given precious promises by the Lord for their faithfulness. To the overcomers at Ephesus, Christ says: "To him who overcomes I will give to eat from the tree of life, which is in the midst of the Paradise of God" (Revelation 2:7). This, of course, is a promise of eternal life in the future Kingdom, but I also believe that the Lord "feeds" us His life even now in the form of spiritual nourishment to help us survive and triumph in this dark and fallen world. Once we leave the tree of the knowledge of good and evil and refuse to decide for ourselves what is right and what is wrong, depending always on the will and verdict of the Lord, we are "fed" from the tree of life.

The Bible, the Word of God, and Christ are all referred to as "bread" (John 6:35) and the taking of Communion, properly discerned, is also spiritual sustenance (John 6:55). Our spirits as well as our bodies must be fed and nourished for us to complete our journey with Christ and be well-pleasing in His eyes.

The overcomers in the church in Smyrna are promised "He who overcomes shall not be hurt by the second death" (Revelation 2:11). The second death refers to the lake of fire in which all those not found in the Book of Life will spend eternity, along with the devil, the beast (Antichrist), false prophet, Death, and Hades (Revelation 20:11–15). Many of the believers in Smyrna would indeed suffer the "first" death for their faith, but Christ assures them that they would spend eternity with Him, safe and secure from all future suffering.

The faithful believers in Pergamos were given this promise: "To him who overcomes I will give some of the hidden manna to eat. And I will give him a white stone, and on the stone a new name written which no one knows except him who receives it" (Revelation 2:17). Hidden manna and a white stone with a new name written on it: what could these be?

In Roman times, a white stone was often given as the price of admission to certain events. Perhaps, the white stone Christ refers to is the "ticket" to the Kingdom. Also, in the days of Rome, white stones with the victor's name on it were awarded to the winners in athletic events, and the stone served as the means to take part in the award banquets. The new name in Christ's promise to the overcomers at Pergamos (and to us) is probably some unique aspect of a believer's victory in the Lord, or it could be the Lord's new name. Whatever the white stone and new name might mean, they are something very personal, even intimate, to each believer and are, therefore, to be highly prized.

Many interpretations of the hidden manna have also been offered through the years. We know that a pot of the manna from the Israelites' forty years in the wilderness during the days of Moses was placed in the Ark of the Covenant, and some Bible scholars believe this is the hidden manna of Revelation 2:17.

Others think the hidden manna is doing the will of the Father and being faithful to finish the work of the Lord till He comes, even as Christ did during His earthly sojourn (John 4:32–34), hence, a spiritual meaning. In John 6:55, Christ declares that His flesh is real food and His blood real drink. *Real* in what sense? Spiritually. The taking of the Lord's Supper, properly understood, strengthens the spirit and weakens the flesh. Again, regardless of what the hidden manna actually is, it is something we should all highly desire and treasure and will be the reward for the overcomers in this life.

Thyatira was the church with the worst faults, corrupted on many fronts. But the overcomers at Thyatira were also given great and precious promises for their faithfulness: "And he who overcomes, and keeps My works until the end, to him I will give power over the nations'—He shall rule them with a rod of iron; they shall be dashed to pieces like the potter's vessels'—as I also have received from My Father; and I will give him the morning star" (Revelation 2:26–28).

Power to rule and reign with Christ during the millennium will be the main reward for the overcomers at Thyatira and in all ages since. The second condition was to "keep His works until the end"—what exactly is meant here? The key word is *His*—to be so tuned in to the Lord and His will that only *His* works are done, not the works of the disciple (no matter how well-intentioned), but the Lord's work alone. Christ is the source, the means, the results, and the glory of all efforts in His name.

But what is the morning star that the Lord promises to give? Most scholars believe that it refers to Christ Himself (2 Peter 1:19 and Revelation 22:16). Of course, spiritually speaking, all believers already "have" Christ, but when He returns, we will have him fully, both spiritually and physically, never to be without Him again! We will see Him as He is and share eternity with Him. What a promise! In the skies, it is the appearance of the morning star that breaks through the darkness of the night. Thus, will Christ be at His second advent: "There shall be no night there: they need no lamp nor light of the sun, for the Lord God gives them light. And they shall reign forever and ever" (Revelation 22:5). Hallelujah!

Those who remained faithful and overcame the obstacles at Sardis were given this promise by the Lord: "He who overcomes shall be clothed in white garments, and I will not blot his name from the Book of Life; but I will confess his name before My Father and before His angels" (Revelation 3:5).

The white garments stand for purity, remaining unstained, which the Lord declares makes them "worthy" (verse 3:4). And the "blotting out" of names from the Book of Life is an interesting term to consider as well. Some scholars think names are added to the Book of Life as individuals come to Christ in repentance and belief. But I have concluded that everyone ever born was recorded in this Book, for the love of God was and is for the whole world and all of its people. Names are only removed or "blotted out" when someone dies without ever coming to Christ. I do not believe it has anything to do with being saved, added to the Book, and then losing that salvation, thereby having their name expunged. Rather, the removal of a name is the result of never coming to Christ in the first place.

In spite of their lukewarm condition and being oblivious to their true need (as a church), there were still overcoming believers at Laodicea, who were also given promises by the Lord: "To him who overcomes I will grant to sit with Me on My throne, as I also overcame and sat down with My Father on His throne" (Revelation 3:21).

Charles Dickens opened one of his well-known novels with the words, "It was the best of times, it was the worst of times" (*A Tale of Two Cities*). That is a perfect description of the church in Laodicea and of much of the church today. Christ made that clear with His declaration of wishing they were either cold or hot rather than lukewarm, about to be vomited out of His mouth! Spiritually speaking, being hot or cold is much better than being lukewarm: being hot is what the Lord desires from His disciples and is, therefore, a good thing. Being cold, especially reaching the "bottom" temperature, can be used by the Lord to arouse a true but complacent believer back to his senses; he can be convicted by realizing just how far he had fallen and repent. But lukewarmness is a comfort zone where the flesh can keep reassuring its victim to just relax, that everything is just fine (like being immersed in a dark tank of perfectly regulated water, the mind and heart overcome by the surrounding comfort).

That, I believe, is the condition of the overall church in America today. It mirrors exactly what happened to Israel before judgment fell on the Northern Kingdom in 722 Bc and then on Judah in 586 Bc. Israel had been so richly blessed spiritually and materially during the reign of Solomon that its people became lukewarm toward God and most things spiritual. As He always does, God sent forth warnings of impending disaster again and again, which, of course, went unheeded. Like today, prophets and true ministers of the Lord were either ignored or discredited.

We too have forgotten both the source and the requirements of our blessings; first the requirements and conditions for continued blessings and then the very source itself. Little by little, God and the true Christian faith are being banished from this country. Warnings have been sent forth by God: verbally by men of God, by economic crises, by terrorist attacks, by increased natural disasters and signs in the heavens, by false teaching, and by caving in to charges of "intolerance" if we do not compromise the truth and include all religions being of God (although Christ Himself said there is no other way to God except through Him). We have gone to sleep! The church in America should be on its face in repentance, begging for God's mercy and long-suffering to continue while we try to awaken and praising Him for withholding judgment for as long as He has! Anything else is just another form of the status quo, humming to ourselves sweetly as we snooze, ensuring the full weight of judgment sooner or later.

I did not intend to digress (if indeed *that* is what I did), but if we do not learn from history, the Bible, or Israel and its downfall, what are we to do but expect the worst?

Returning to the church in Laodicea, the Lord gives a very long introduction or lead-up to the His promise to overcomers: "As many as I love, I rebuke and chasten.

Therefore be zealous and repent. Behold, I stand at the door and knock. If anyone hears My voice and opens the door, I will come in to him and dine with him, and he with Me" (Revelation 3:19–21).

The great love of the Lord for all of us is the reason we are rebuked and chastened. Unbelievers are warned again and again before their eternal fates are sealed. Believers, likewise, are rebuked and chastened before judgment is executed. The Lord knocks and knocks, but it is we who must respond and open the door! Eventually, in all cases, if His cries of love go unheeded, judgment must follow; His mercy and long-suffering must end. Did they repent at Laodicea? I have been unable to find an answer to that question. But even more important is this question: will we awaken and repent?

The promise given to the overcomers at Laodicea is a great one: to sit on His throne with Him! He overcame as a man, securing our salvation, and was seated by the Father on His throne in the heavens, and overcomers in this life will join Him there! This promise does not only apply to those in Laodicea who repented but also to those throughout the church age (including us) who hold fast to the true gospel of our Lord.

Why have I concluded that the seven churches in Revelation 2 and 3 are a true representation of the entire church age? The reasons are many, but I will only include a few here. The number one reason is the incredible parallel of the conditions of the seven churches to the conditions through which the church as a whole has passed. The similarities go well beyond coincidence or stretching the scriptures to fit history: they go hand in hand.

The other two reasons I have come to this conclusion are from the Bible itself. All the churches in Revelation 2 and 3 are told "He who has an ear, let him hear what the Spirit says to the churches" (Revelation 2:7, 11, 17, 29; 3:6, 13, 22). *Churches*, plural, not simply the *church* He was addressing. He meant the other six and all the churches that followed.

In Revelation 21:7, Christ declares, "He who overcomes shall inherit *all* things, and I will be His God and he shall be My son." In this passage, the Lord is describing the new Jerusalem, the new heaven, and the new earth. All overcomers from all the ages of the church will inherit all things! The main obstacles to overcome are the faults Christ condemns in the seven churches of Revelation—all products of "some other gospel"—robbing believers of their true identity and full inheritance in Christ.

Will we learn from the lessons of both history and the Holy Scriptures? There is yet time to repent and return to the true gospel and worship of God; judgment can be averted. I find myself caught between two extremes: I desire for the church to awaken and for a great revival and restoration to sweep the land, but I long even more for the second coming of Christ and the establishment of His

Kingdom for this fallen earth to be redeemed and all things to be made right. Could both of these incredible events occur simultaneously? An awakening and a final revival, one that would usher in the King? As I said earlier, these are the best of times and the worst of times, even as it was at Christ's first advent. Critical mass for some earthshaking move by God seems near.

One thing I do know: it is time for the true people of God to put their houses in order, to draw closer to the Lord than ever before, to empty their lives of all "leaven" and renew their commitment to our God, and to steer clear of the spirits of this age…thus says the Spirit. Let all who have ears hear and obey!

Are All Believers Overcomers?

THIS HAS BEEN a much-debated question, especially more recently in church history. Many think that all believers are overcomers, having overcome judgment and hellfire by the sacrificial death and grace of our Lord. Certainly, judgment and eternal separation from God are procured by true faith in the death of Christ in our place. We overcome because He overcame and paid for our sins. But this is a free gift, by grace, with nothing required from us to obtain except repentance and belief. But once saved, isn't there anything for us to overcome ourselves, not as a means to salvation but as a result of our conversion? Most would agree that there is; it has even been given a name: sanctification.

The web site GotQuestions.org defines sanctification as coming from the same Greek word as holiness, *haggios*, meaning "a separation." First, it was a once-for-all positional separation unto Christ at our salvation; second, a practical, progressive holiness in a believer's life while awaiting the return of Christ. Third, we will be changed into His perfect likeness—holy, sanctified, and "completely separated from the presence of evil."

It is from the positional separation unto Christ at our salvation to a practical, progressive holiness that overcoming (or not overcoming) comes into play. Some continue to make this transition throughout their life in Christ, while others do not, hence, both the wise and the foolish virgins in the parable of Matthew 25. To be "wise" and continue to make *practical* progress in the process of sanctification, continual sacrifice of self must be offered up, our will completely surrendered to His will *no matter what*. Such a life brings pain and suffering to the flesh, which is why many are not willing to live in this manner.

Also, most start down the wrong road after their salvation experience. I certainly did. I went from resisting God and willfully sinning to trying my very best to go the other way, not realizing that I was doing it in my own power. I read and studied the scriptures, gleaning what I should do (and often succeeded), but I always came up short at some point. So I would repent and redouble my efforts to do better, to "be like Christ," conformed to His image.

But failure always awaited me sooner or later. And it took many such failures (and the frustration and guilt that accompanied them) before I began to see I was still on the same road as I had been before coming to Christ, the only difference being that I was striving to do "good" instead of evil. And the Holy Spirit, at this point, began to show me that such a way was completely impossible. I was then indeed "ripe" for a new revelation from the Spirit of God.

While reading a book by Watchman Nee one day, I ran into his experience with Romans 6, especially verses 6 and 11: "Knowing this, that our old man was crucified with Him, that the body of sin might be done away with, that we should no longer be slaves to sin" (6:6).

"Likewise you also, reckon yourselves dead indeed to sin, but alive to God in Christ Jesus our Lord" (6:11). I immediately realized that all my former efforts to be like Christ were the works of my *old man*, the man who was supposed to be dead!

It took some time before I learned how my *new* man was to live and proceed, but little by little, I began to make progress. As I stopped trying to decide a course of action to be taken in certain situations and exercising my own will to accomplish the results I thought the Lord desired, the struggles and failures were replaced by peace and success. There were certainly more bumps in the road ahead, and the need for yet more revelations from the Holy Spirit to go through the hard spots that were waiting, but I knew I was on the right path, eating from the tree of life. I will save the explanation of those *other* needed revelations for Part 2 of the book. For now, returning to the original question (Are all believers overcomers?), I would answer that in the negative. Some never leave the tree of death (the apt name for the tree of the knowledge of good and evil), continuing to learn some new lesson or doctrine that might help them improve their behavior but never finding the way to consistent success. Others get on the right path but, at some point, are not willing to sacrifice their own will for the will and life of Christ; such a way just seems too painful, or the enemy deceives them into believing that such a sacrifice is not even necessary.

All believers are *called* to be overcomers, but some do not fully answer that call. And for those who think *all* believers *are* overcomers, at least two important points must be remembered: first, Christ addressed all believers at each of the seven churches and made a distinction between those who were failing to overcome and those who had remained faithful (overcomers) in spite of the widespread following of "some other gospel." *And only the overcomers were promised blessings and rewards in the coming Kingdom.* The rest were told to do one thing: repent! Second, all ten virgins in the parable of Matthew 25 were believers, as evidenced by being called *virgins* and being given oil (representative of the Holy Spirit). The only difference was that five were foolish and five were wise. The foolish were excluded from the Marriage Supper, the wise included (even, I think, making up part of the bride).

Any charge that the five foolish ones were never really saved in the first place, the preceding paragraph disproves. And to say that they were indeed saved ones who had lost their salvation by misbehavior is, likewise, erroneous because salvation is by faith alone and not based on works.

The "practical, progressive" process of sanctification was passed by the wise but failed by the foolish.

If you are a true believer in Christ, leave the doomed path of the tree of the knowledge of good and evil, trying to please God by simply "doing better" in your own power. The old man cannot be rehabilitated; he was condemned to die—he and all the vestiges of his life! Begin each day by surrendering your will to Christ and ask the Holy Spirit to keep you on *that* path throughout the day, no matter what circumstances may arise. Ask for forgiveness when you fail, get up and go on, allowing the Holy Spirit to do His work in you, conforming you to the image of Christ. For this is the price of being an overcomer, of ruling and reigning with the Lord in the coming Kingdom…and this is the *true* gospel.

The Church in America Today

SOMEONE WE KNOW, who was dissatisfied with her church, asked my wife one day, "But if I leave my church, how will I know which one is right and which one I should attend?" That is such a good question (and a condemning one as well). There are so many! My answer would be that there are none who have it *all* "right." I have often said that when Christ comes and we get our "report card" grading our understanding of the scriptures, no one will receive a 100A+ (hence, the need and importance of always remaining teachable).

As far as which church to attend, I would advise anyone asking that question to find a church that believes the Bible is the inerrant Word of God, where there is a fervent desire to understand the Word, allowing the Holy Spirit and the life of Christ to teach and lead. A church or gathering that will allow Christ to be Christ and not one in which men lead the way, waiting (and waiting, if necessary) for the Lord to come forth whether it be in teaching, praying, worshiping, or moving out into the community with the good news and labors of love. Unity will reign, and such a place will have the blessings of God upon it.

The churches in America today include all the traditional Catholic and Protestant denominations and variations, nondenominations, interdenominations, as well as recent attempts to move away from the traditional (parachurch group organizations). There are also a growing number of believers now gathering and worshiping in small home groups, independent of any organizational oversight. This is all the result of division caused by the infusion of "some other gospel" (many others) and attempts to return to the true one. There is some truth in most of these attempts to worship and follow the Lord, but division of the Body of Christ has weakened the true witness of His gospel. The result? Satan continues as the prince of the power of the air, and the coming of Christ is delayed. And we quibble over the smallest of things! There are some differences that make no difference one way or the other, and other differences that the Holy Spirit could clear up if we would allow Him to, remaining teachable and open to His direction, even as they did at the council in Jerusalem (Acts 11).

Broader categories such as *evangelical* (and, of course, *non-evangelical!*) and *charismatic* are common today in the American church. Wikipedia defines those two categories in this way:

> Evangelicalism is a worldwide Protestant movement, maintaining that the essence of the gospel consists in the doctrine of salvation by Jesus Christ's atonement. The movement gained

> momentum in the eighteenth and nineteenth centuries with the emergence of Methodism and the Great Awakenings in the British Isles and North America...

And, of course, included in the beliefs of evangelicalism are what they believe concerning the Bible, God, law, man, Jesus, forgiveness, repentance, works, inheritance, and deception, each of which is given scriptural support. Studying through the list, I find that it is very difficult to find anything in which to object; but the problem is that others do find those things and, hence, become non-evangelical (even *beyond* evangelical). So the well-intentioned desire to return to the true gospel of Christ (necessary because of all the divisions) only seems to have resulted in more labels and division!

The same holds true in the charismatic movement. Wikipedia defines it this way: "The Charismatic Movement is a trend in Christianity distinguished by its belief in the renewal of supernatural gifts and powers."

Of course, some charismatics might also be evangelical, and some evangelicals might be charismatics, but others oppose one another in their beliefs, hence, more division and weakness in the Body of Christ.

As far as the need for the renewal of supernatural gifts and powers, they only diminished due to "some other gospel"—the gospel of men. Christ said that believers would do even greater things than He did because He was going to the Father (John 14:12), and He gave us all authority over all the power of the enemy (Luke 10:19). Whether they are still *normative* or not (the explanation of some for their decreased manifestation), they should still be more fully in operation and part of what Watchman Nee called "the normal Christian life."

What always must be remembered is this: life is more important than doctrine. It is certainly essential to study the scriptures and listen to the Holy Spirit as we come to important conclusions as to what we believe and what is not of God, but we also must remain teachable during our journey with the Lord. To set down everything in the form of doctrines or creeds is, by its very nature, exclusive (if one does not believe those things, he cannot be included in as a brother in the Lord), and many times doctrines are "set in concrete" long after the Spirit and life of the Lord have departed from a true move of God.

The brethren in England once denied fellowship with Watchman Nee because he had broken bread and taken the Lord's Supper with some other group. Did Brother Nee cease being a true disciple of Christ for such an action? Certainly not. He went on to manifest more of the life of Christ than almost anyone of whom I am aware. A true disciple of Christ—that is all any of us should aspire to be. Any label beyond that is unnecessary and divisive.

Easy Believism and the Prosperity Gospel

EASY BELIEVISM AND the so-called prosperity gospel are two other prevalent features to be found in the church today, not only in America but worldwide. So much of the gospel of the American church has been "exported" to the rest of the Christian world. We will discuss these two teachings one at a time.

It has become a widespread practice to invite unbelievers to just accept Jesus and be saved. "Accept Jesus"—that term or phrase has always bothered me. First of all, it appears nowhere in the Bible, and secondly, it should be the other way around, being overjoyed that Jesus accepts us! After this invitation (or something similar), would-be believers are told to just invite Jesus into their heart to become their personal Savior. Again, this is not scriptural; I can't find anything in the Word that backs it up. We are actually called to be part of the Body of Christ, not a personal friend of the Lord, not just me and Jesus.

Worse yet, seldom is the need for repentance mentioned in such evangelistic approaches. And while I know such methods are well-meaning and meant to win souls to the Lord, without repentance, there can be no salvation. Just reciting a prayer or inviting Jesus into your heart does not get the job done. We must repent as well as believe. Leaving repentance out becomes an easy believism unwarranted by the Lord or His Word. Countless souls who have followed this "formula" and not come to repentance later on face the real possibility of not being saved at all.

Some ministers of the gospel would say that repentance add works to salvation, and that we are saved by faith alone. But repentance goes hand-in-hand with belief because Christ is to be Lord as well as Savior of our lives. In fact, to believe in Jesus includes believing what He taught, which was to repent and believe (John 4:17 and elsewhere). This was well understood in the early church, but in more recent church history, the Lordship/Savior issue has become quite controversial.

Without repentance, many who think they are saved feel no need for any major changes in their lives. They may attempt to be better on some fronts, but on others they continue to sin, with no check from their conscience at all, excusing themselves as just "being human." Such lives no doubt partly account for the overall spiritually anemic condition of the modern church.

But if Christ is not Lord, He is not qualified to be Savior! To me, that seems to be a no-brainer. And if He is Lord (and He is), that means I must do as He says; I have no say in the matter. That starts with repentance, for He commands it in many passages in the Word. And after being saved, we no longer have the right to make independent choices. The Scripture clearly states that we who believe are no longer our own, for we were bought at a great cost (1 Corinthians 6:19–20). Just to believe that Christ is the Son of God is not enough; even Satan and his demons know and believe that.

John MacArthur wrote a book a little over twenty-five years ago titled *The Gospel According to Jesus*. I just finished reading the anniversary edition and am in total agreement with its basic premise. Mr. MacArthur is so concerned for the souls who think they have become Christians via this easy belief-only approach, but are not converted at all, and will face eternal damnation thinking they are truly saved. The book clearly shows that such a teaching is "some other gospel" and not the true gospel at all.

If anything, Jesus portrayed truly believing and following Him as a most difficult undertaking. He warns us to carefully "count the cost" (Luke 14:26–30) before coming to Him as a disciple, for in the end, it will cost us everything of the flesh and its earthly lusts and desires (even some that seem legitimate and normal, like love of family: our love for Him must come first, ahead of love for anything and anyone else, Luke 14:26). Indeed, if we read the words of Jesus carefully, we find that He discouraged, even condemned, half-hearted commitment, demanding total submission from any who desired to be His disciple.

Wikipedia defines the prosperity *gospel* as a "Christian religious doctrine that financial blessings is the will of God for Christians, and that faith, positive speech and donations to Christian ministries will increase one's personal wealth."

The prosperity message was birthed in the 1940s and 1950s, post-war era. Revival and tent meetings swept across the country, where the *seeds* of this doctrine were planted. In the 1960s, it gained momentum by the rise of the televangelists, appealing especially to the poor and impoverished. Megachurches sprang up, and the prosperity message dominated both radio and television. The message became an integral part of the Word of Faith movement of the 1970s; this doctrine teaches that faith, and positive words actually bring into existence both good health and financial blessings (some have called it the "name it and claim it" gospel). In more recent history, divine healing and financial well-being have been prominent in the teaching of what is called the charismatic movement. And, of course, there has been a widespread dissemination and acceptance of all these ideas abroad, gaining strong followings around the world (especially in Third World countries).

The problem with this gospel is that it rests upon false assumptions, the stretching of the scriptures, and, in some cases, the temptation toward greed. While it is quite true that God desires to bless His people, those blessings are not promised to always be of a financial nature. First and foremost, we have been blessed with the forgiveness of sins and the privilege of spending eternity with Christ; beyond that, being part of a new creation, conformed to His image, a new race of mankind (as the Father originally intended). And we are promised to be partakers of His divine nature! What could be better than that?

Christ said that in this world, we will have tribulation (John 16:33) and that to be His disciple means suffering for the sake of the gospel, even as He suffered for doing the will of the Father ("A disciple is not above his teacher, nor a servant above his master. It is enough for a disciple that he be like his teacher, and a servant like his master. If they have called the master of the house Beelzebub, how much more will they call those of his household!" Matthew 10:2–25). We live in a fallen world that is broken (and as a good brother puts it, "a lot more broken than we know"). If we truly live for Christ, we can expect the prince of this world to oppose us in any way that the Lord allows.

When it comes to money, we must remember that monetary value placed upon everything is of the devil; he has "trafficked" in everything from fine goods to the souls of men (Revelation 18:11–13). With God, though He owns "the cattle on a thousand hills" (Psalm 50:10) and all the gold and silver, He operates by grace. We must have enough money and goods to survive and do the work of Christ, but anything beyond that is, again, up to the Lord. I believe He wisely bestows upon each believer what each can handle, some given more because they will use it well and not be corrupted by it; others less for providential reasons we may or may not understand.

The wisdom of Agur in Proverbs 30 seems the very best attitude for any believer to adopt: "Give me neither poverty nor riches—Feed me the food allotted to me; Lest I be full and deny You, and say, 'Who is the Lord?' Or lest I be poor and steal, and profane the name of my God" (verses 8 to 9). The "food allotted to me"—that is the key; what God has decided is best for my growth and His glory. Beyond that, no more prosperity should even be desired, and certainly, giving to get is a motive of the flesh and "some other gospel."

Conclusion of Part 1

So MANY OTHER issues causing divisions exist in the church today: speaking in tongues, divine healing, the working of miracles, the role of women, just to mention a few. But rather than discussing them all, let us be content to know that the result has been to weaken the church, thereby, robbing believers of our true identity and full inheritance in Christ (perhaps, even delaying the return of the Lord). The attempts to recover the true gospel have, for the most part, only created more divisions!

So what are we to do? Do all we can to recover the true gospel! But in the process, endeavor not to cause more division. That must be our course as individual believers and as members of the Body of Christ. Now let us proceed and see where that search will take us.

PART 2

RECOVERING THE TRUE GOSPEL

Soul and Spirit

Men have made the Gospel of Christ so complicated! Why is that so? Certainly, the enemy of our souls has been at work, for he delights in confusion and the distortion of the truth. But the main culprit has been ourselves. Deception must find a place to be planted and to flourish. Without that place, there is nowhere that lies can take root and grow. That necessary fertile ground is in the very soul of man!

I have discussed the need for the separation of soul from spirit in all of my previous books. It is essential that we understand this truth before we can even begin to recover the true gospel. It was this revelation many years ago that ended my frustration and guilt from all my failed attempts at being like Jesus. Conforming believers to the image of Christ is the task of the Holy Spirit, but without dividing soul from spirit, His job is impossible.

Listen to what Paul says in Hebrews 4:12: "For the word of God is living and powerful, and sharper than any two-edged sword, piercing even to the division of soul and spirit, and of joints and marrow, and is a discerner of the thoughts and intents of the heart." It is the Word of God wielded by the Holy Spirit that must do this crucial surgery! At first,

I did not quite understand what was involved here. I had never known that the soul and the spirit are two distinct parts in the makeup of man.

I decided that if it is the Word of God that must perform this work, I would find the answers to my questions surrounding soul and spirit right there in the Word. So I studied and prayed and then prayed and studied. Reading the works of Watchman Nee, especially *The Spiritual Man*, alongside the Bible helped immensely. I began to see that, indeed, soul and spirit are not one and the same. The message in 1 Thessalonians 5:23 confirmed this for me; Paul, in the closing of his letter, says: "Now may the God of peace Himself sanctify you completely; and may your whole spirit, soul, and body be preserved blameless at the coming of our Lord Jesus Christ." All three parts listed separately!

So like God Himself, in whose likeness man is created, we are a three-part being. Once I understood and accepted this, I needed to better understand what the functions of those three parts are. The body with its five senses is obviously required for meaningful contact with the world around us: we are able to see, hear, touch, smell, and taste the wonders of our environment. The soul, on the other hand, is primarily for meaningful contact with ourselves and those with whom we interact—its faculties include the mind, the emotions, and the will (the ability to choose). But what about the spirit?

To understand the function of the spirit, the Lord led me back to what happened in the Garden of Eden, when man decided to go his own way. Before sin entered, Adam and Eve walked and talked with God, but after that first transgression, they were expelled from the garden and the presence of the Lord, cut off from direct, two-way communication. As I prayed to better understand what happened that day, the Lord led me to John 4:24: "God is Spirit, and those who worship Him must worship in spirit and truth."

I began to see that our spirit is necessary for any meaningful relationship with God—from His Spirit to our spirit and from our spirit to His. This alone is true worship.

So in Eden, man's spirit was still operational, thereby enabling him to commune with God. But something terrible happened when that first sin was committed: the spirit of man, the part of him designed for contact with God, became nonfunctional, as though dead, and he was cast from the presence of God with only his own soul to direct his life, deciding for himself what was right and wrong. The worst consequence of the Fall was, indeed, the severing of Spirit-to-spirit communication with God.

I already knew that the salvation experience includes a quickening to life of the spirit (being "given" a new spirit as well as a new heart). All of the above made it very clear to me that the function of the spirit is for the purpose of communing and worshiping God; it was "dead" to this function before salvation but then made "alive" to it after repentance, belief, and conversion to Christ. The natural life of man, when unconverted, is controlled by the soul (what the individual thinks, feels, and decides), independent from God; the soul is in charge, which is what the tree of the knowledge of good and evil is all about. After salvation, the spirit is to lead, receiving from God through the Holy Spirit and the Word the choices to be made. The soul is to become the steward of the spirit, carrying out the will of God.

The problem, however, is that the soul has been in control for so long; it does not relinquish its role of leading the way so easily. Most new believers simply try to correct their old ways, resisting sinful choices and endeavoring to make good ones instead. Many old habits indeed are overcome, but sooner or later, it becomes obvious that something is wrong: certain sins, attitudes, or ways of thinking hang on and keep tripping them up. It takes many such failures for most believers to realize they simply can't do it. Some just give up and "do the best they can," thinking that is all that is possible. Others read all the incredible things the new creation is to include and persevere in seeking the path to such a life. Such a seeker is indeed ripe for the revelation of spirit-soul division, for Matthew 5:6 promises, "Blessed are those who hunger and thirst for righteousness, for they shall be filled."

The next thing the Holy Spirit taught me is the meaning of the word *flesh* in Scripture. We tend to think of it in physical terms only—how tall we are, the color of our eyes, the size of our hands, et cetera, but in reality, flesh includes everything we were born with naturally. The only part this excludes is our spirit, for at our natural birth, our spirit was essentially nonexistent, not functioning, and as though dead. Our soul with its mind, will, and emotions, on the other hand, was very much a part of our natural makeup and, therefore, is included as flesh in the scriptural use of the term. That being the case, whatever originates from the soul or is empowered by it can never produce spiritual results, for John 3:6 states quite clearly, "That which is born of the flesh is flesh, and that which is born of the Spirit is spirit." In other words, like begets like.

Paul tells us in 1 Corinthians 15:31, "I die daily..." By this, the apostle means he allowed the Cross to cut away and "kill" portions of flesh that hindered the process of spirit-soul division (which gets us back to *sanctification*; for it is this daily "dying" to self that allows the Spirit's sanctifying work to progress). O that we all might come to understand and submit to this critical work! For it is the only way back to the true gospel.

It is difficult to recall the exact order of the revelations from the Holy Spirit in my quest for more of God. But what I do remember is that somewhere along the way, I began to see that the lack of this spirit-soul division accounts for much of the division the enemy has been able to inject into the Body of Christ. No matter how well-intentioned we are, if we operate from the soul in spiritual endeavors, differences, discord, and division are bound to occur—and indeed have.

If, for example, a brother in the Lord and I disagree on something and we have both been broken to the degree that the humility of Christ has been released into our lives, we can take the disagreement to the Holy Spirit in prayer, and He will give the correct understanding and answer to our issue. But if, on the other hand, spirit and soul have not been adequately divided, we will both continue to believe that our point of view is the right one and may decide to split and go opposite ways. This is exactly what has happened in so many cases throughout the church age.

The church's strength is in its unity, truly being one in the Spirit, and living the true gospel of Christ. Divided, we are no match for Satan. Ephesians 4:1–6 states this so beautifully: "I, therefore, the prisoner of the Lord, beseech you to walk worthy of the calling with which you were called, with lowliness and gentleness, with long-suffering, bearing one another in love, endeavoring to keep the unity of the Spirit in the bond of peace. There is one body and one Spirit, just as you were called in one hope of your calling; one Lord, one faith, one baptism; one God and Father of all, who is above all, and through all, and in you all." Without brokenness and the dividing of soul from spirit, this is impossible!

Repentance

"How long will you slumber, O sluggard? When will you rise from your sleep? A little sleep, a little slumber, a little folding of the hands to sleep—so shall your poverty come on you like a prowler, and your need like an armed man."

Proverbs 6:9–11

"So I sought for a man among them who would make a wall, and stand in the gap before Me on behalf of the land, that I should not destroy it; *but I found none.*" (Emphasis mine)

—Ezekiel 22:30

"There was a little city with few men in it; and a great king came against it, besieged it, and built great snares around it. Now there was found in it a poor wise man, and he by his wisdom delivered the city. Yet no one remembered that same poor man."

—Ecclesiastes 9:14–15

> "If my people who are called by My name will humble themselves, and pray and seek My face, *and turn from their wicked ways,* then I will hear from heaven, and will forgive their sin and heal their land." (Emphasis mine)
>
> —2 Chronicles 7:14

The need for repentance is a good place to start in our discussion of recovering the true gospel. Repentance is essential for the obtaining of salvation and continuing to live a life that is pleasing to the Lord (for short of sinless perfection, it will always be needed on this side of the Kingdom). In recent times, in an effort to attract potential believers, repentance has been downplayed, or even not mentioned at all. Some have erroneously come to believe that adding the need for repentance in the process of salvation is adding works to the faith by which we must be saved. Just believe, they teach.

But throughout the New Testament, the words given are to repent *and* believe. John the Baptist came preaching repentance, as did all the early apostles as well as Christ Himself, so how can this great need be omitted and called what transpires true conversion? For is not repenting part of the belief and faith in Christ required for salvation? Jesus came to forgive sin and save sinners from condemnation, granting them regeneration or new birth and the promise of eternal life; the sinner must believe this to be true and acknowledge their sin and be willing to turn from it. Anything less seems to me to be compromising the true gospel.

Not only is repentance required on a personal basis, but also on a corporate level. When the people of God go astray to "some other gospel" or fall into false worship and habitual sin, it takes deep repentance for God to forgive and restore them to fellowship and blessing. The nation of Israel experienced this process again and again in its history—first, the falling away from true spirituality followed by conviction of their sins and then repentance and restoration. In some cases, however, harsh judgment fell because they would not repent, and judgment was not lifted until repentance came.

The church has gone through similar periods, and it has taken desperate, heartfelt repentance for revival of true worship to return. We are in just such a place now! Much of the church seems to be asleep, going through the motions of spirituality, attending services, and giving token attention to God, but little else. True holiness is a rarity; Christ being given full reign of one's life is talked about more than actually lived.

And worst of all, perhaps, so few realize the depths to which we have fallen! I wrote a short poem recently called "The Sedative of Comfort," and that is a good description of where we are, spiritually speaking, in the American church—overtaken and put to sleep by the abundance of comfort and blessings we enjoy, exactly the condition in the Laodicean church of Revelation 3:14–22. We are in desperate need of the "eye salve" of the Spirit, that we might see and then allow self to be purged and refined by the Spirit so that we might be clothed with purity (white garments). But what will it take to awaken us—a great catastrophe, going into exile, and captivity by our enemies (even as did ancient Israel)?

The Lord will not withhold His hand of judgment forever. I am amazed that it has not fallen already. I often plead with Him to extend His mercy, grace, and long-suffering just a little longer, giving the church the time it needs to awaken and repent. But just how long such prayer will continue to avail, I do not know. Many I speak to and try to arouse to cry out to God in repentance agree that our spiritual condition has sunk to extremely low levels, but the same ones are not willing to make a sustained effort in prayer to bring about healing. Some excuse themselves (after all, we go to church, help the poor, are good parents, obey the law, etc., etc., etc.); this excuse is mostly unspoken but easy to detect by attitude and lukewarm responses.

Others say they just don't "have a burden" about those kind of things. That was the answer I got from one friend as I wept over legalized abortion. She said she thought it was a terrible, but she just wasn't as moved over the issue as I am. What do you say to something like that? How can anyone not feel deeply over the killing of innocent unborn children? Nothing could be worse than that in my estimation; any people who will legally take the life of the unborn are capable of committing any conceivable atrocity known to man. The shedding of innocent blood was repeatedly condemned by God in His Word, followed by swift and harsh judgment if the warnings to cease went unheeded.

Watchman Nee taught me many valuable points concerning prayer. The first cautioned against superficial prayers, not staying in prayer on a particular need until the release of the burden by our spirit, and instead just mentioning the issue briefly and then quickly skipping to another one. I liken such prayer to skipping flat stones across a wide pond with none of the missiles ever reaching the other side. Granted, there are so many things to pray about, but we should learn to listen to the Holy Spirit as to which ones are on the heart of God during that specific time of prayer and then pray accordingly and for as long as the burden remains.

Brother Watchman also said that at any particular gathering of the Body for corporate prayer, we should limit the topics of prayer to two or, at most, three areas of concern. This should help lingering over each prayer long enough for the Holy Spirit to signal our spirit that we have covered the topic adequately and can move on to another. I have attended many prayer meetings in which we prayed over a vast array of true needs, moving from personal ones to others all around the world! Such an approach is certainly well-intentioned but may not make any real change in the situations addressed.

This gets us to another valid point to consider: Nee's idea of a "prayer net." By this, he meant enclosing a prayer around a need so securely with as many angles covered as the Spirit suggests and then cinching up the net so tightly the enemy cannot find a way in to "undo" what has been prayed. To do this, of course, again requires waiting on the Spirit to finish all He has to say on the subject and not speeding off to another item, leaving the first one "unprotected" against the intrusion of the devil! The last suggestion our Chinese brother made covers both individual and corporate prayer. He said our times in corporate prayer in terms of topics and intensity should not exceed those we have prayed in our private prayer closet before coming together with our brothers and sisters for body prayer. This should encourage us to spend more time than most of us do in personal prayer, and by limiting ourselves when we meet corporately, there will be more time for others to pray for what they receive from the Spirit.

I realize that the last three paragraphs briefly left the topic of repentance, but I felt that the Lord wanted me to include them; I hope that they have been helpful. In regard to repentance, it is my firm belief that the need is so great. Repentance needs to be central in our times of prayer, both personally and corporately. In fact, it is my prayer that prayer groups everywhere would set aside times to pray for nothing else, not to the exclusion of meeting for other purposes at other times but also not neglecting how urgently prayer for repentance is needed.

The scripture 2 Chronicles 7:14 is a much quoted verse during times of spiritual decline in which the need for revival and restoration is so great. I have heard many messages based on its contents—very good ones—but I noticed that the fourth point ("turn from their wicked ways") is seldom elaborated upon; in fact, when I hear it quoted aloud, that part is often left out altogether. Humbling ourselves, praying, and seeking the face of the Lord are certainly essential elements to such a prayer, but so is the repentance implied at the conclusion of the verse.

There are many "wicked ways" a people can fall into, bringing spiritual malaise and the judgment of God upon themselves. Certainly, the obvious ones should be repented of, with a firm commitment not to return to such practices. But there is also one that is not so obvious but is a very serious transgression: falling into "some other gospel," the very purpose for writing this book. Most all believers, especially those in more recent church history, have been guilty of this sin. In the majority of cases, it has been committed unwittingly—believers haven't ever known anything else and have come to believe that is all there is to the gospel.

But once the Holy Spirit opens our eyes to the truth, it is imperative that we repent both for ourselves and the

Body of Christ, making every effort to move on to the true gospel of Christ. This is so critical!

I could have written this chapter where it is or at the beginning of Part 3, "Living by the Indwelling Life," but either way, we must see and respond to this monumental need of the church. For unless we do, I do not see anything else that will correct our current impotent condition and restore us to the power and glory God intends for us. Beyond that, nothing else will turn away certain judgment.

In the rest of Part 2, "Recovering the True Gospel," we are going to explore the revelations of the Holy Spirit that will get us back on the right track and leave all other "gospels" behind. But for now, I want to say a bit more about repentance to encourage you to get started on it. Don't get discouraged if you cannot find many to join you. Zechariah 4:10 tells us not to despise small beginnings: "The hands of Zerubbabel have laid the foundations of this temple; his hands shall also finish it. Then you will know that the Lord of hosts has sent Me to you. For who has despised the day of small things? For these seven rejoice to see the plumb line in the hand of Zerubbabel. They are the eyes of the Lord, which scan to and fro throughout the whole earth."

Ecclesiastes 9:5 testifies to the same truth: *one* poor wise man saved a city besieged by a king (it makes no difference if the man was remembered by other men; God certainly noticed). Evan Roberts prayed for revival for over thirteen years before the Great Awakening broke forth in the British

Isles and then North America. I am sure others prayed too, but what a commitment and perseverance! (Roberts worked for twelve hours a day as a coal miner, getting buried in the bowels of the earth and doing little else but praying the rest of the time. One day, a friend ran into Evan and said, "Brother Evan, we have not seen much of you lately. What have you been doing?" Roberts answered, "Praying the Kingdom.") O Lord, raise up such men and women today! You say in Psalm 110:3 that in the day of Your battle, You will have Your children of a willing heart. Surely, such days are upon us, so send them, Lord!

Now let us move on to the ways of recovering and living the true gospel of our Lord and Savior.

Crucified with Christ

> "How shall we, who died to sin, live any longer in it? Or do you not know that as many of us as were baptized into Christ Jesus also were baptized into His death? Therefore, we were buried with Him through baptism into death, that just as Christ was raised from the dead by the glory of the Father, even so we also should walk in newness of life. For if we have been united together in the likeness of His death, certainly we shall also be in the likeness of His resurrection, knowing this, that our old man was crucified with Him, that the body of sin might be done away with, that we should no longer be slaves of sin… Likewise you also, reckon yourselves to be dead indeed to sin, but alive to God in Christ Jesus our Lord."
>
> —Romans 6:1–6, 11

I REMEMBER SO well when I first understood what Paul was saying here. I had been in despair due to my repeated failures to *imitate* Jesus and live a life of holiness. My understanding of this passage in Romans came while reading Watchman Nee's book, *The Release of the Spirit*. At first, what these verses say seemed completely incomprehensible. The rational mind of my soul was still very much in operation, and, of course, it objected. How could I have been crucified *with* Christ over two thousand years ago? How is such a thing even possible?

Of course, it did not take long for the Lord to show me the answer. He directed me to Ephesians chapter 1 where Paul declares quite eloquently that all who belong to the Lord have been *in* Him from "before the foundation of the world" (1:4). That too was met with objections from my mind: I not only was chosen and placed in Christ, but this all happened before the foundations of the world were laid? The Spirit answered my question in the affirmative—yes, absolutely!

As I sat marveling at such a fact, still not really understanding, the Lord made what should have been very obvious clear: He is not limited to time and space! He can do anything and at any time He so desires. Therefore, placing me in Christ centuries and centuries before I was born presented no problem to Him whatsoever. And I had already been convinced that no one who is truly saved can ever lose that salvation.

So when I read Brother Watchman's illustration of being "in Christ" as a permanent condition, it was quite easy to believe Romans 6. He used the simple picture of placing a letter in a book and shipping it somewhere or wrapping up the book and placing it on a shelf for an indeterminate period of time. Without any outside interference, the letter would still be in the book. So being in Christ from before the foundation of the world and nothing able to take us out, we are still in Christ and in Him at the time of His crucifixion! So when He died, so did our "old man"—that fallen, sinful man dominated by his own soul.

When Christ was raised, so were we (Romans 6:5), and when He ascended, so did we (Ephesians 2:6)! For wherever He is and has been, we are and have been! A careful reading of Ephesians reveals that everything we have and everything we are is due to the fact of being in Christ (verses 7, 10, 11, 13). Of course, all of this must be appropriated by faith, believing what God has said. But then, all that we have as believers in Christ must be accepted by faith for them to become reality for us.

So as I began to walk in the light of this new revelation, I was so excited. I was sure I had found the answer to all my previous failures and dilemmas. But it wasn't long before my newfound enthusiasm was dashed. I believed what the Lord had shown me, and I tried to "reckon" it so (Romans 6:11). But I still kept failing. In fact, at times, my old man seemed to be more alive than ever before! There continued to be a disparity between my position in Christ and my experience of that position. Romans 6 and many other passages in Scripture (which the Spirit pointed out very clearly) told me who I am in Christ, but I still did not know how to live out that position.

A Mystery Revealed

> "I now rejoice in my sufferings for you, and fill up in my flesh what is lacking in the afflictions of Christ, for the sake of His body, which is the church, of which I became a minister according to the stewardship from God which was given to me for you, to fulfill the word of God, the mystery which has been hidden from ages and generations, *but now has been revealed to His saints.* To them God willed to make known what are the riches of the glory of this mystery among the Gentiles: which is *Christ in you, the hope of glory.*" (Emphases mine).
>
> —Colossians 1:24–27

THE ILLUMINATION OF this passage by the Holy Spirit became for me the key to making the transition from the *position to the experience* of our identity in Christ (not only knowing who we are but also living it). I realized that not only are we, as believers, "in" Christ but that He is in us as well, and that Him in us is "the hope of glory." Paul says in the Colossians quotation above that this was a mystery hidden throughout the ages until it was revealed to him so that he might reveal it to us. I was already aware of the words of Christ found in John 15:5, that without Him, we can do nothing. But I always thought that meant we should pray for Him to help us, to be with us in our time of need. With better understanding of the indwelling presence of Christ, revealed in the above quoted passage, I began to suspect that there is more to it than that.

It wasn't long after that revelation that I was led to consider verses like Colossians 1:17–19, 3:11, and I read Watchman Nee's book, *Christ the Sum of All Things Spiritual*. I gradually began to see that God's eternal purpose is that His Son would be all in all and the sum of all things; that outside Christ Himself, there is nothing spiritual. And since He is in us, He must be allowed to be all things spiritual in us. He does not teach us truth so that we can apply what is learned; *He Himself is truth*. He is the way and the life—did He not say so in John 14:6? And He corrected Martha in John 11:25, saying that He Himself *is* the resurrection, not that one day He would perform resurrection by raising from the dead those who believed upon Him.

Little by little, I was beginning to see the true gospel, and it was much simpler than men had made it to be. It was not a myriad assortment of "things" and doctrines. It was not the imitation of Christ by even the most sincere efforts at holiness. Holiness is Christ, and the only way for us to be holy is to allow Him to come forth. Jesus told the rich young ruler that none but God is good; I just had not realized the full implications of what the Lord meant.

It is not for us to be humble, to strive for peace in our life, gentleness, or to do the *right thing*, or anything else spiritual. Christ *is* all of these things; outside Him, they simply do not exist!

So the logical conclusion I came to is that the true gospel is Christ, and to live as He commanded us to live is only possible by Him being released and manifesting His life. And for that to happen, we must get out of the way. Of course, this gets back to Paul's declaration that he "died daily." But how do we die daily? That was the question with which I was left.

The Trigger of Life

Most students of the Bible know Jesus said more than once that He only did the will of the Father, and that He said we could do nothing without Him. So the central importance of the will began to take shape in my mind. The soul is the pivotal point between the body and the spirit; in it come the decisions of life, which way we will choose to go—God's or our own. The will is in the center of the soul, so in a very real sense, it is the "trigger" of life. The mind and emotions have their parts to play in making those choices, but in the end, it is the will that chooses.

So when Jesus continually surrendered His own will to the will of the Father, only the will of God came forth. Likewise, when Paul died daily, what was required was the submission of his will to the will of Christ. Of course, neither Paul nor we can make that perfect submission in every circumstance. At times, our own will definitely manifests; otherwise, sinless perfection would be possible while yet in this body of flesh. But quick heartfelt repentance gains forgiveness in such cases and restores us for the decisions that come next in our life.

The will of God in most situations we will face are to be found in the Bible, His written Word. That is why it is so critical that we know the Word. And the Holy Spirit can and will reveal His will "on the spot" when we do not know from His Word what we should do. All the Spirit requires is our sincerity and willingness to follow His will once He reveals it. By growing closer and closer to the Lord in all aspects of our life, we are much more apt to "hear the Spirit" when His voice is so needed. Spending extended periods in prayer will also enhance our knowing of the will of God. I am convinced that much of the time when Christ went aside to pray was spent seeking and listening to the will of His Father. We should set aside such times regularly for the same purpose.

I have come to believe that when I surrender my will to the Lord, it frees His will and life to come forth. It is not that I just sit idly by while He does something. On the contrary, often action on my part is called for, but when it is the will of Christ in what I do, I have peace and the assurance that the results the Lord desires will be accomplished, whether they be immediately or in the Lord's timing.

An Exchanged Life

ALL OF THE foregoing raises a very interesting question: is living in the way just described a changed life or an *exchanged* life? I first encountered this distinction when reading about the life of Hudson Taylor (1832–1905). Mr. Taylor was a medical doctor and missionary to China, founding what became known as the China Inland Mission. For many years, he struggled with the same issues concerning the Christian life with which I had wrestled: how to live a truly holy life, one that is pleasing unto God.

He too had failed again and again, redoubling his efforts in prayer, fasting, reading the Word, and serving those around him selflessly; but they were all to no avail. Yet he persevered! Hungering and thirsting for true righteousness, the Spirit, in due time, filled him. He came to realize that all of his previous efforts, as well-intentioned as they were, were worthless and not even necessary—"filthy rags" as they were. All at once, he knew that all he had to do was rest in what Christ had already done and filled him with, to simply surrender his own will and soulish efforts, and the life within him would manifest. And it did!

The following is an excerpt from *Hudson Taylor's Spiritual Secret* by Dr. and Mrs. Howard Taylor:

> It was resting in Jesus now, and letting Him do the work—which makes all the difference. Whenever he spoke in meetings after that, a new power seemed to flow from him, and in the practical things of life, a new peace possessed him. Troubles did not worry him as before. He cast everything on God in a new way, and gave more time to prayer.
>
> It was an *exchanged life* that had come to him—the life that is indeed 'No longer I'… It was a blessed reality 'Christ liveth in me.' And how great the difference!—instead of bondage, liberty; instead of failure, quiet victories within; instead of fear and weakness, a restful sense of sufficiency in Another.

I truly believe this to be an accurate description of what the Christian life is to be all about; it certainly describes my own experience. So many believers go down the path of a *changed* life, consciously or unconsciously seeking to improve the old man or making the mistake of taking the new man down the same dead-end way of self-improvement. Neither method is the way of the true gospel. In the process, the gospel of Christ is "dumbed down" and becomes "some other gospel," a powerless detour created by Satan and the soul of man.

Other Bible scholars disagree with the idea of an exchanged life; they prefer to call it an "imparted life." And certainly, Christ has imparted His life to us, but in the process of using that impartation, there is an exchange that takes place—our will for His will, releasing His life. I think the problem is one of semantics: Hudson Taylor came to see that the attempts at merely a changed life (trying to choose the good and avoid the bad) was doomed to failure and not the true gospel at all; that it took the life of Christ being released for victory to come. That does not mean that Christ does the work *instead* of us, that we are just passive bystanders. The will of Christ most often requires action on our part, but the life that empowers it is the life of Christ; He does the work *through* us.

I have yet to read any other objections that convince me that Mr. Taylor's and my own experience are invalid, or even worse, not scriptural. I certainly have not reached my final destination in following this path (perhaps, that will not even occur while yet here on earth in this body of flesh), but I believe I am on the right track. I too have experienced many breakthroughs and areas of victory that before seemed inaccessible.

In Part 3, I plan to explore the subject of learning to live by that indwelling life, which is what must be accomplished if the true gospel of Christ is to be lived out. But before going to that discussion, we need to better understand what it means to enter (and live) in the rest of God.

Resting in God

In Hebrews 3 and 4, Paul discusses the subject of resting in God. In chapter 3, Christ is presented as our model of faithfulness. Then Paul brings up the case of the children of Israel after they were delivered from Egypt under the leadership of Moses. He uses them as an example of failing to enter the rest of God, and even gives the reason in verse 19 of chapter 3: unbelief. Chapter 4, verse 2 repeats the reason for their failure: "For indeed the gospel was preached to us as well as to them; but the word which they heard did not profit them, not being mixed with faith in those who heard it."

Paul's concern was for believers then and now, that none should miss entering the rest in God (*still* available) for the same reason: the sin of unbelief, the failure of faith in the words of God. So that we would understand what he meant by this rest, Paul gives an interesting explanation: he goes all the way back to the creation story in Genesis.

Referring to the seventh day of creation, when God rested from His work of the other six days, Paul begins his analogy: "For He has spoken in a certain place of the seventh day in this way: 'And God rested on the seventh day from all His works'; and again in this place: 'They shall not enter My rest'" (Hebrews 4:4–5). This in spite of what Paul said at the end of verse 3: "Although the works were finished from the foundation of the earth."

Putting this altogether, we come to understand what Paul was saying: once all had been created and God declared that what He had done was "very good" (Genesis 1:31), He was able to rest in that established fact and reality. His omniscience knew that no matter what mankind and Satan did to undo His perfect plan and creation, it would come to pass just as He had conceived and designed it. And *this* is what we, as believers, must rest in as well; again, no matter what the enemy and circumstances do to dissuade and discourage us, if God has said it, it is certain! This is what we must build our Christian life upon.

Verses 9 and 10 of this chapter give us the key to entering God's rest. After reassuring us that such a rest still remains, the apostle says: "For he who has entered His rest has himself also ceased from his works as God did from His." The works of believers to which Paul is referring are the works of the soul, works of the flesh—works that originate in the mind of man instead of in his spirit or works that begin in the Spirit but that the flesh gets involved along the way. Such works produce no true fruit and are easily infiltrated by the enemy. All such efforts must be abandoned to enter the rest of God.

The entire nation of Israel failed to enter God's rest in spite of their miraculous deliverance from Egypt and divine intervention on their behalf again and again. Paul gives this warning so that we might not fail as well. And, of course, in the midst of his exhortation is the need for soul and spirit to be divided (4:12) to the extent that even the "thoughts and intents of heart" are fully surrendered and resting in the words and promises of God. For nothing can be hidden from Him to whom we must "give account" (4:13), and resting in God is only possible when this crucial division is allowed to take place.

Revivals

DUE TO THE proliferation of "some other gospel," the need for revivals has become commonplace. Since any other gospel is no gospel at all, the waning of true life has created this need. And certainly all efforts in this direction have been well-intentioned. In the first church where I taught and preached, there were two revivals "scheduled" each year, one in the spring and one in the fall. But even then, I realized that true Holy Spirit revival cannot be scheduled. It is born of deep repentance, even desperation, from Spirit-starved believers, usually when the majority of the people of God have grown complacent, taking the blessings of God for granted and giving the Lord only token attention and worship.

But when even a remnant of the faithful cry out, God will answer with a fresh inflowing of His Spirit. This has happened many times in both the Old and New Testament. After seventy years of captivity in Babylon, the Lord heard the fervent prayers of the prophet Daniel and delivered the children of Israel once again. The Great Awakening in the British Isles and North America in the eighteenth and nineteenth centuries was conceived and birthed by repentance and prayer.

There are those today crying out again, for the "temperature" for much of Christiandom has become lukewarm (especially in the British Isles, Europe, and North America—the very locations of the Great Awakening). Why does the great need for revival arise again and again? There are actually several reasons, but I would like to discuss only one.

So much of the true gospel has been changed or lost that a complete renewal is needed. But revivals of the past have tended to turn on a single deviation the Holy Spirit wishes to correct or, at most, a few points of departure from the true gospel. This being the case, all previous revivals have followed what I call a bell-shaped curve: the rising of the Spirit and reception by believers on the left side of the bell, a crescendo reached at the top of the arc and then a descent down the right side of the bell as the movement "cools" off or becomes derailed by the souls of those involved.

Disagreements and debates grow up based on various aspects opposing believers think should be stressed. Or after the Holy Spirit moves on, attempts to "capture" or reduce to a formula what has been essential to bring the revival about in the first place emerge. What follows crystallizes into new doctrine, is usually given a name, and in the end results in yet more division!

Today we are, indeed, in deep need of revival! But the revival I long for is what I call the *final* revival—a revival that will not end, a revival that will usher in the King, a revival birthed by the few willing to allow Christ to be Christ, those who are so "sold out" that they have sacrificed their own will to the will of Christ and have lived by the indwelling life of the Lord. For this is the only thing the Father, Son, and Holy Spirit want from any of us. And the good news is that He will get it (Psalm 110:3)!

Before Going On

Before proceeding to Part 3, *Living by the Indwelling Life*, let's summarize what we have discussed up to this point. As I said before, the revelations of the Holy Spirit in our search for the true gospel of Christ do not have to come in any particular order; they will, no doubt, vary considerably in the experiences of all seekers of the truth. But all the essential points of understanding must be given by the Holy Spirit and the believer's spiritual path corrected accordingly. For me, the revelations have come as following:

1. Struggling mightily to live as Christ commanded;
2. Realizing that some gospel other than the true gospel has been created by Satan and the souls of men, the result being weakness and division, robbing believers of their true identity and full inheritance in Christ;
3. Being shown that all my previous efforts at holiness were the work of the "old man," empowered by my own will and strength, the parts of me that were to have "died" with Christ at His crucifixion;

4. The realization that man is a three-part being—spirit, soul, and body; the body for contact with the world around him, the soul for consciousness of self and interaction with others, and the spirit for communion and worship of God. Being shown that "flesh" is anything we are born with naturally, including the soul as well as the body; that the soul on its own can never produce true and lasting spiritual fruit; that the soul is the seat of power in the natural man, the spirit to take that position in the redeemed; that the spirit is essentially nonfunctional until regeneration, being quickened to life by the Holy Spirit at the moment of repentance and belief in Christ (what is commonly called being "born again");

5. The need for soul and spirit to be divided by the Holy Spirit, the Word, and the work of the Cross. Only by this operation can it be said that a man is truly spiritual;

6. Comprehending what it means to have been "in Christ" since before the foundation of the world, thereby establishing the believer's position of belonging to the Lord and a joint heir with Him;

7. Seeing that Christ Himself indwells all true believers, "Christ in us, the hope of glory," and that by submitting to His will and power, His life is released so that our position in Christ might become our experience as well;

8. That the eternal purpose of God is for His Son to become all in all and the sum of all things, everything in all creation, beginning with man, filled with nothing but the life and glory of Christ;

9. Coming to see that the true gospel and all things spiritual come down to one thing: Christ;

10. Due to all the foregoing (plus many other supporting details gleaned along the way), we must learn to live by the indwelling life of Christ—an exchanged life—for this is how the true gospel manifests itself.

PART 3

LIVING BY THE INDWELLING LIFE

Inheritance and Dominion

> "And I will pray the Father, and He will give you another Helper, that He may abide with you forever—the Spirit of truth, whom the world cannot receive, because it neither sees Him nor knows Him but you know Him, for He dwells with you and will be in you."
>
> —John 14:16–17

> "The mystery which has been hidden from ages and from generations, but now has been revealed to His saints…which is Christ in you, the hope of glory."
>
> —Colossians 1:26 and 27

WHEN WE READ the Sermon on the Mount (especially the Beatitudes), it becomes very clear that no one can live such a life except Christ Himself. For in the Beatitudes, Jesus describes the very nature of those who will rule and reign with Him in the Kingdom; these are the *overcomers*, those mentioned as the heirs to the precious promises in Revelation 2 and 3. These are they who have made Christ all in all in their lives, in full submission to His will and life in all things; the wise virgins. They will not only rule with Christ in the Kingdom but will also come into their full inheritance in Christ while yet on earth; in fact, it is only by having come into it that they become overcomers.

But what is our full inheritance in Christ? Certainly, ruling with the Lord when He returns is part of that inheritance, the reward for overcoming in this life. But what are the blessings we should inherit now to be lived out after our salvation? What has Christ's great victory over Satan, sin, and death yielded for all believers on this side of the Kingdom? There are many promises in the scriptures that point to various aspects of our inheritance (which define our true identity—who we are in Christ). But the most inclusive of them all is to be found in John 14:12: "Most assuredly, I say to you, he who believes in Me, the works that I do he will do also; and greater works than these he will do, because I go to my Father."

Did you get that? Greater things than Christ Himself did! Heal the sick? Give sight to the blind? Drive out demons? Raise the dead? We know that these and other miracles do yet occur from time to time but not very often; they seem to be the exception and not normative. The Lord also gave us another clue in that verse: doing even greater things is possible because "He went to His Father." What could that possibly mean?

As I pursued an answer to this question, the Holy Spirit reminded me to always remember that Jesus came as a man and that he overcame as a man. He is certainly and eternally

God as well, but He emptied Himself of His divine attributes when He came to earth to bring salvation. Philippians 2 makes this very clear (although, of course, there has been much debate over this portion of Scripture). Oddly enough, it was originally presented as a hymn, and the problem concerns trying to reconcile Christ's dual nature of being both God and man—the God-Man, some have called Him (I suppose capitalizing the M in *man* helps satisfy some, for He, indeed, was the perfect man as well as eternal God).

And knowing some will also object to this next statement as well, I, nonetheless, believe it true. By coming as a man, Jesus accepted certain limitations inherent in man. He could not be in two places at the same time, for example; He could not suddenly vanish; and most important of all, He was mortal. He would have to die not only as atonement for our sins but also simply because He was a flesh-and-blood human being.

But what about *after* His death, burial, and resurrection? All limitations were gone! He could be everywhere at once, He could pass through solid walls, and death could never touch Him again (nor will it ever touch us again once we have been clothed in our glorified bodies like unto His own). The apostle John informs us in his first epistle that we too shall have all these glorious benefits when Christ returns: "Behold what manner of love the Father has bestowed on us, that we should be called the children of God! Therefore the world does not know us, because it did not know Him.

Beloved, now we are the children of God; and it has not yet been revealed what we shall be, but we know that when He is revealed, we shall be like Him, for we shall see Him as He is" (1 John 3:1–2).

Hallelujah!

But again, what about now here on earth? What limitations have been removed because Jesus died for us, was raised, and went to His Father? To answer that question, we have to ask, how was it Jesus could do the things He did as a man? He is ever our example. First of all, He never sinned. In our case, however, there is sin, but all is forgiven each time we repent. So the sin issue does not seem to be the full answer to the power of Christ. What is it then?

Submission to the Father in all things—this was the source of His power. Jesus spoke of His dependence upon the will and life of God the Father more than once. In John 5:30, He said, "I can of Myself do nothing. As I hear, I judge; and My judgment is righteous, I do not seek My own will but the will of the Father who sent Me." In John 6:38, we find these words: "For I have come down from heaven, not to do my own will, but the will of Him who sent Me." And in John 14:10, Christ said, "Do you not believe that I am in the Father, and the Father in Me? The words that I speak to you I do not speak on My own authority; but the Father who dwells in Me does the works." So by full surrender to the will of the Father, the life of the Father was released to do the work and the miracles Jesus performed.

In the metaphor of the vine and branches, John 15:5 declares these words: "I am the vine, you are the branches. He who abides in Me, and I in Him, bears much fruit; for without Me, you can do nothing." Is this not the answer to our question? Jesus did the things He was able to do because of the submission of His own will to the will of the Father. Likewise, we are empowered by the submission of our will to the will of Christ. In both cases, the divine life is released to do the works.

What happened when Jesus went to His Father? He was enthroned next to God the Father and was given the Holy Spirit to pour out on all those who would believe in Him throughout the ages! And by faith in Christ and the indwelling of the Holy Spirit and the Lord Himself, we become a new creation (2 Corinthians 5:17). Again, hallelujah! But this raises yet another question: what is this new creation spoken of here?

The original creation—the "old" one—was ruined by sin; it became far less than what God intended. But remember, God "rested" that seventh day, the setback caused by Satan and sin He knew was only a temporary setback; all things would eventually be exactly as He had planned. Part of that plan was to give man dominion over all of creation (as well as His Son being all in all, of course). Genesis 1:27–28 tells of this desire of the Father: "So God created man in His own image, in the image of God He created him; male and female He created them. Then God blessed them, and God said to them, 'Be fruitful and multiply; fill the earth and subdue it; have dominion over the fish of the sea, over the birds of the air, and *over every living thing that moves in the earth*'" (emphasis mine).

But the "fall" of man subverted God's intention: the spirit of man became nonfunctional, his soul the "headquarters" of his life, and his dominion lost to the enemy, Satan, who became the prince of this world, the old creation. From that time forward, God began looking for the man He intended all mankind to be. Many "good" men came and went throughout history, but none of them was the man God was looking for. But at long last, that man appeared: Jesus!

The scriptures that make that so clear are Psalm 2:7–9, a prophetic psalm, and Hebrews 5:5: "So also Christ did not glorify Himself to become High Priest, but it was He who said to Him: 'You are My Son, today I have begotten You.'" This was not spoken at Bethlehem at Christ's natural birth; it was not spoken until *after* the resurrection! Do you see what that means? The Father finally had the man He had been looking for! He had defeated Satan, sin, and death and regained the dominion Adam had lost to the enemy. And He is a "life-giving" spirit (1 Corinthians 15:45), indwelling all who repent and, by faith, receive Him. He, indeed, is the progenitor of a new race, the firstborn from the dead, with many brothers and sisters, those who share His spiritual DNA, for like begets like!

We are joint-heirs with Christ (Romans 8:17) now and into all eternity. The dominion lost to Satan has now been regained—did not Christ Himself say to His disciples, "Behold, I give you the authority to trample on serpents and scorpions, and over all the power of the enemy, and nothing shall by any means hurt you" (Luke 10:19)? That means, of course, that many of those limitations and restrictions imposed by the old order of things are now no longer binding. We are now partakers of His divine nature, the riches of our inheritance in Christ!

Without the life of Christ being released, the Body of Christ has been left vulnerable to the deceptive tactics of the enemy. He has been able to infiltrate and motivate the souls of men to do spiritual work, which has led to the production of "some other gospel," thereby weakening and dividing believers. As we have already discussed, periodic revivals have restored some truth and power to the church, but they have also caused more divisions once the revival has ended. The true gospel is Christ Himself, the embodiment of all things spiritual. Let us now pursue this all-important key: learning to live by the indwelling life of Christ. This is certainly largely uncharted territory, discovered and lived by so few during the church age. So if we stumble a bit as we try to walk in this way, don't get discouraged; know that we are on the right path and that the Lord will pick us up if we fall (for the culmination of His great plan is more important to Him than it is to us).

A Beginning

I HAVE TAUGHT these truths for some time, and those who hear the teachings all ask the same question: but how do we *do* it? We are so accustomed to methods and formulas for making spiritual progress, so many steps of how-to! Unfortunately, living by the indwelling life of Christ cannot be reduced to such a procedure. With the help of the Holy Spirit, it is simply "letting Christ be Christ." It is the Holy Spirit who reveals and releases the life, and it's the Holy Spirit who will let us know when we have failed to yield our will to the will of Christ (when it is *us* once again, in other words). Beyond that, it is growing closer and closer to the Lord and desiring His will above all things. As it says in the Lord's Prayer, "Your kingdom come, Your will be done on earth as it is in heaven" (Matthew 6:10).

It is the "how-tos" that have caused so many divisions in the Body of Christ. Our need for steps leading to a desired end provides a perfect outlet for the soul to become involved, leading the way, stifling the voice of the spirit. So many books have been written with "formulas" for life in the Spirit. (I hope this one of mine doesn't fall into the same category!)

In Part 2, we discussed the meaning of resting in God. We must repeat the necessity of that way of life, for it is a prerequisite for living by the indwelling life of Christ. But even before learning how to rest in God, we must have come to "the end of ourselves"—a deep knowledge and acceptance of our own inadequacy in spiritual matters, not only that the "old man" was crucified with Christ but also that the "new man" cannot succeed by staying on the road leading from the tree of the knowledge of good and evil any better than the old one did. We must truly know that Christ *in* us, the hope of glory, is our *only* hope for victory and indeed is the very way for us to live as believers in the Son of God.

Paul tells us in Hebrews 4:10 that "He who has entered His rest has himself also ceased from his works as God did from His." Of course, what is being said in all of this is that we must "die to self"; if we do, only then will our soul cease trying to lead the way or add its input along the way in spiritual work. In Matthew 10:38–39, Jesus said, "And he who does not take up his cross and follow after Me is not worthy of Me. He who finds His life will lose it, and he who loses his life for My sake will find it." The word for *life* here is *psuche*, the same word for *soul* or *soul-life*. This part of us must be put in its proper place, never initiating or directing but only following the Holy Spirit via our spirit.

Such a believer as just described is more than ready to rest in God, knowing that He will bring about all He has planned and spoken in terms of both personal and corporate promises. Because God has rested in that fact, so can we. No matter what the enemy brings against us or the Body of Christ, the will of God shall prevail! We must settle that in our own hearts… and what a place to reside!

Once we truly begin to rest in God, not asserting our own will and power, the life of our indwelling Lord is released to work in whatever way He chooses. That is when these promises are so precious and powerful: "At that day you will know that I am in My Father, and you in Me, and I in you. He who has my commandments and keeps them, it is he who loves Me. And he who loves Me will be loved by My Father, and I will love him and manifest myself to him…If anyone loves Me, he will keep My word; and My Father will love him, and We will come to him and make Our home with him" (John 14:20–21, 23). Manifesting Himself to us and making their home with us—how could that reality be made any clearer? And how can anything be more glorious?

Living in Community

AND IT IS certainly necessary to live this out in community as part of a Body dedicated to the same purpose; no one can succeed on their own. In recent months, I have allowed myself to become much too isolated, not attached to any particular gathering of believers. I knew this to be a detrimental position in which to be (having seen other brothers do the same thing), and the enemy likes to get us one-on-one, a place where we are no match for him. To be properly fed by the Lord, we need one another, and by being mutually filled, we are better able to function as a whole Body, an expression of Christ on the earth; for this is the ordained way of God for all believers.

The problem, of course, is finding even a small group who will come together with no agenda or program, waiting for the Lord to come forth and express what He wants to do that particular day. Perhaps, it will be nothing but praise and worship; at other times, nothing but prayer for what concerns Him; still other times may be for teaching what He wants us to learn. We must simply wait upon the Lord, but waiting upon Him is extremely difficult for most of us. What if nothing happens while we wait? Many have asked this question, and my answer is, "So what?" We will have waited and listened, which truly pleases the Lord. Just listening and loving Him is a great exercise for all of us to practice more.

If we are having difficulty finding a group who will gather in this spirit, we should pray that the Lord will send a few. Unfortunately, the tendency is to become more isolated than we should allow to occur, so at all costs, avoid a prolonged period of isolation. Perhaps, there is a spouse or close friend who will join us; numbers are not important. Did not Jesus say that where two or three are gathered in His name, He would be in the midst? Such a gathering is a great desire of the Father, so I am sure He will send others; the key is simply to get started.

I am at that point right now—I have a new "ministry" in mind (if we must call it something). But before I discuss that, I would like to pause and speak of all the influences the Lord will send our way if we continue to be teachable and desire His will. The Lord has always been very good at supplying me with exactly what I need next; the only requirement on my part has been to keep hungering and thirsting for more of Him and walking in the light of what He has already sent. Meeting just the right person, being directed to the perfect book, or just fresh surges of new revelation—He has been so faithful giving me the next step in my walk.

Certain believers, especially those who have recorded their experiences in the Lord, have been immensely helpful.

One such brother is Watchman Nee (1903–1972). One day many years ago, a friend handed me his book, *Love Not the World*. I was amazed by what I read and knew I had found a "kindred spirit." His understanding of Scripture and many of his experiences in the spiritual life paralleled my own. I next read *The Spiritual Man*, a three-volume set written by Watchman when he was in his early twenties and had been told by doctors that he was dying of tuberculosis (he was later miraculously healed by the Lord).

Again, total amazement! How could one so young know and live at such a deep level in the Spirit? I later found out that *The Spiritual Man* was the only book Watchman ever actually wrote himself; the rest were written by the transcribing of notes by those who heard his teachings. One Christmas, my wife found over fifty titles by Watchman and gave them to me as a gift. Boy, was I delighted (and kept busy reading and studying for a very long time). Another brother in the Lord who has more recently come alongside is Frank Viola. I have read most of his books and teachings and subscribe to his blog. I have found both help and great encouragement by "meeting" Brother Frank. The last book of his which I read is called *God's Favorite Place on Earth*. The title intrigued me, and I knew a real treat was waiting for me inside!

The book was written as a narrative by Lazarus concerning his experiences with the Lord. Mary and Martha were the sisters of Lazarus, and Simon the leper his father. The family resided in Bethany, their house a place where Jesus often visited on His way to and from Jerusalem and other destinations. Viola identified Bethany as God's favorite place on earth and then proceeded to explain why.

The word Bethany has two meanings: house of figs and house of the afflicted. Both fit perfectly in the context of the story—Simon the leper was an afflicted one healed by the Lord, and figs are quite significant in both testaments, relating to the nation of Israel. In fact, the fig tree is often used as a symbol of the country itself.

Christ's cursing of the fig tree in Matthew 21:19 when He was returning from Bethany to Jerusalem was His indictment of the nation and the Law. In Luke 13:9, the parable concerning the fig tree and its unfruitfulness after more than three years of hard work, again, is a picture of Christ's ministry among the Jews: no fruit had been produced. Jesus was about to end His ministry and be crucified, so also the end of His efforts with His own people. The cursing of the fig tree and the old ways it represented was His final verdict on the failure of the Law to produce righteousness.

But Bethany, especially the household of Simon the leper, was a place of great fruitfulness; the "figs" there were ripe and plentiful. Bethany was where Christ was always welcomed, loved, and allowed to be Himself. As a result, all who were there were blessed—Simon healed from his leprosy and his son raised from the dead! It was in Bethany where Christ could feed and be fed Himself; that is why Viola called it God's favorite place on earth.

And Christ is yet looking for a Bethany today—many of them, in fact, places where the afflicted and those who are well due to His miraculous intervention into their lives can meet, worship, love Him and one another; where He feels completely "at home"; where the agenda of man and soulish efforts are left outside; and where worshiping "in spirit and truth" is allowed to be in full operation.

This is what has been on my heart for some time now: a Bethany House—not a church or rehabilitation center but simply a gathering of those who love the Lord, willing to defer to Him in all things, and to submit to one another, each supplying his or her part to the Body of Christ, that His Life might truly be made manifest in the earth. And I believe this has been the Father's heart ever since the resurrection of His beloved Son (and even before then, of course).

All would be welcome to come—believers who have hungered for a deeper walk with the Lord and unbelievers in desperate need of deliverance from some addiction or demonic activity in their lives. I believe that if we will just fully submit to the Lord's will, miracles will again become commonplace. God is the same yesterday, today, and forever: He yearns to save the lost and set the captives free! Again, it was a book by Watchman Nee that caused me to realize how far below our inheritance as children of God that we are living. The name of the book is *The Normal Christian Life*. What should be normal has almost disappeared, and we have contented ourselves with spiritual crumbs! Is it not time that we eat from the full and sumptuous meal the Lord has prepared for us?

Simplifying

> "And I, brethren, when I came to you, did not come with excellence of speech, or of wisdom declaring to you the testimony of God, for I determined not to know anything among you except Jesus Christ and Him crucified. I was with you in weakness, in fear, and in much trembling. And my speech and my preaching were not with persuasive words of human wisdom, but in demonstration of the Spirit and of power, that your faith should not be in the wisdom of men but in the power of God."
>
> —1 Corinthians 2:1–5

My grandmother made sure I attended church as a boy. I never really questioned what I was taught about God and Christ, but I never had a conversion experience either. When I went away to college, I did begin to question my early exposure to spiritual matters. I explored other religions and the philosophies of men and thoughts of the great thinkers, finding it all very interesting but never completely satisfying. I always went away with a deep desire to keep looking.

Finally, while working as a night clerk in an Austin, Texas motel, I had a truly miraculous experience with the Lord (no need here to go into detail, but the Holy Spirit definitely gave me an epiphany of the Deity of Christ). After a rather prolonged period of resistance to what I had been shown, I was saved and actively began pursuing the Christian life.

And, of course, that meant sorting through the myriad of beliefs the church has become. I was like a hermit crab, trying on a particular shell that seemed to fit for a while but then finding I had "outgrown" it (finding some limiting factor or point of doctrine) and moving on to another one. This went on for several years with many frustrations and seeming dead ends before the Lord began to show me that such a search was entirely unnecessary; that all the different "shades" the church had become were due to the works of the flesh, well-intentioned but misguided attempts to reduce the glory of Christ to a list of many things and doctrines, the making of methods or systems by which to live the Christian life.

In short, I saw that the true gospel of Christ is much simpler than we have made it and that by complicating it, we have reduced it to the efforts of human wisdom, thereby robbing it of its power and glory. Paul speaks quite clearly of that danger in 1 Corinthians 2:1–5. Though blessed with a brilliant mind and superior religious education, Paul endeavored to know and to teach one thing and one thing only: Christ and Him crucified! By doing that, the Spirit and the life of Christ were released in great and mighty ways!

Since that revelation, I have committed to following the same path and plan to stay on it the rest of my life. (I often tell people that after trying them all, I am riding a "one-trick pony," but I also add that it is the most important pony and one that very few ride anymore!) It has often been said that even a little child can understand the Gospel, and in Matthew 18:2–4, in answer to the question concerning the "greatest in the kingdom of heaven," Jesus called a little child to Him, set him in the midst of them, and said, "Assuredly, I say to you, unless you are converted and become as little children, you will by no means enter the kingdom of heaven. Therefore whoever humbles himself as this little child is the greatest in the kingdom of heaven.'"

Many sermons have been given on this passage, but I think Jesus was mainly pointing out the simple and humble faith of a child, not complicated by all the questions and doubts that often flood the mind of adults as they try to understand (and live out) the Gospel; pride almost always surfaces in such an approach, pride, and division. So my advice? Simplify, simplify, simplify!

Communion

> "Then Jesus said to them, 'Most assuredly, I say to you, unless you eat the flesh of the Son of Man and drink His blood, you have no life in you. Whoever eats my flesh and drinks my blood has eternal life, and I will raise him up at the last day. *For My flesh is food indeed, and My blood is drink indeed.*" (Emphasis mine)
>
> —John 6:53–55

> "Take, eat; this is My body which is broken for you; do this in remembrance of Me... This cup is the new covenant in My blood. This do, as often as you drink it, in remembrance of Me... But let a man examine himself, and so let him eat of the bread and drink of the cup."
>
> —1 Corinthians 11:24, 25, 28

SATAN'S SCHEMES TO create "some other gospel" have even corrupted the benefits of taking Holy Communion, the Lord's Supper. The early church recognized that this "remembrance of the Lord" is of central importance in the worship of God. They broke the bread and drank of the cup as often as they met. Christ Himself called the bread

(His flesh) and the wine (His blood) "real food and real drink," and unless they ate and drank of it, "they had no life in them." This seems to me to be of more than just symbolic significance.

But what has happened today? One branch of Christianity calls the bread and the wine merely symbolic, and the other says that once blessed, the "emblems" become the actual flesh and blood of Christ. Some churches only "take" Communion occasionally, while others regularly but with an incorrect understanding of what takes place; they gain little value from it. It can even become vain and repetitious, like reciting the Lord's Prayer verbatim (like some kind of holy mantra) over and over without even thinking about what it says and means.

What did Jesus mean when He called the bread and wine real food and real drink? Real in what sense? Answering this question is a key to truly "discerning the Lord's Body" and taking Communion in the right spirit. As humans, we tend to think in dualistic terms (plus/minus, positive/negative, love/hate, etc.), but there is a spiritual reality that transcends this pattern of thought. This spiritual reality is what the bread and the wine of the Lord's Supper are all about. They are *real* on a spiritual plane, and taking them in with this discernment and understanding yields two tremendous benefits—they strengthen the spirit and weaken the flesh! Satan, a spirit himself, well understands this and has done all he can to corrupt and eliminate this source of strength for believers.

A careful reading of the John 6:55 passage tells us the bread *is* real food and the wine *is* real drink; not that they are merely symbols or that they are transformed into the actual body and blood of Christ. So we must take Communion often and in the right spirit; otherwise, we are denied a great source of spiritual strength, inhibiting the release of the indwelling life of Christ.

Another way our enemy has undermined the taking of the Lord's Supper is the Lord's command to "examine" ourselves before we partake. I have known brothers in the Lord who would never take Communion because they still smoked and others who passed it up for other reasons, thinking they were unworthy to take part. But *none* are "worthy" to participate; the whole ceremony is to teach us that Christ alone is worthy. Certainly, pausing before partaking is a time to repent of known sin and to renew our relationship with the Lord, but to skip taking it altogether only serves to weaken such a brother or sister.

Communion is also a time of high praise and mutual sharing with the Lord, praising Him for His great sacrifice and love, rededicating our will to His will in all things, and He, in turn, filling us with an increasing awareness of His life within us. And secondly, it is a time that binds us closer to our brothers and sisters that make up the body of Christ where God has placed us to express His life and image in the earth. Greater unity, love, and sense of purpose are imparted.

Properly discerned and taken, Communion gains so much for the advance of the Kingdom. The enemy suffers loss, and the Kingdom draws a bit closer. Pray with me that the church returns to this mighty source of her strength!

Fruit That Lasts

> "You did not choose Me, but I chose you and appointed you that you should go and bear fruit, and that your fruit should remain, that whatever you ask the Father in My name He may give you."
>
> —John 15:16

> "But the fruit of the Spirit is love, joy, peace, long-suffering, kindness, goodness, faithfulness, gentleness, self-control. Against such there is no law."
>
> —Galatians 5:22–23

FRUITFULNESS IS A much-mentioned topic in the scriptures both in the physical and in the spiritual sense. Israel was blessed with a land that produced lush and plentiful fruit, a great physical blessing of the Lord. It was also to be a place of the bountiful fruit of the Spirit. But Christ's cursing of the fig tree just before He made His final entrance into Jerusalem was His judgment on Israel under the Law: no fruit *that lasts* had been produced. There had been periods of time in their history when *temporary* fruit flourished, times when they had walked close to their God, but decline always followed, and any fruit produced withered and passed away.

In John 15:16, Jesus tells us that He chose us for the very purpose of yielding fruit but fruit that lasts, fruit that will remain. As long as we abide in Him and He in us, this fruitfulness is promised to us. We even have the Father to help us in such an endeavor, who will grant us anything we ask in Christ's name! So we all have work to do!

But what is this "fruit that lasts," and how do we produce it? First of all, as already stated, by abiding in Him and He in us, for it is He who must do the work, His will and His life the necessary ingredients of success. We must, indeed, learn to live by the indwelling life. Fruit produced in any other way will eventually spoil and perish and be judged for what it is—a work of the flesh.

Remember those who will come to the Lord and say, "Lord, Lord, have we not prophesied in Your name, casts out demons in Your name, and done many wonders in Your name?" (Matthew 7:22). Jesus will not deny that they had done the things they mention, will He? But He will say, "I never knew you; depart from Me, you who practice lawlessness" (7:23). They will say three times that all had been done "in His name," and yet Christ was not in it! Just to use His name is meaningless, unless our life backs it up, and any fruit produced in this way will not last.

The only fruit that will last is fruit that will endure through all eternity, first in the coming Kingdom and then into the new heaven and new earth. This fruit alone is imperishable, but what we must always keep in mind is that only the life of Christ can produce such fruit and that no matter what name we give to the fruit to distinguish its characteristics, the fruit itself is Christ! Some will say such statements are too esoteric, mysticism even, but that is only what spiritual reality seems to be to the earthbound mind. If Christ is to be all in all as well as the sum of all things, then *everything* that exists must be filled with nothing but the life and glory of Christ; there is no other way for the Father's eternal purpose to be fulfilled.

What can I say but "Glory! Hallelujah!"

I am sure you have noticed the fruit of the Spirit in Galatians 5:22–23 is singular: love. What we must conclude from this is that love is the only fruit the Father is looking for, and that love expresses itself by the other eight qualities mentioned. And the Word tells us that "God is love" (1 John 4:8). The term *God*, of course, includes the Father, Son, and Holy Spirit, so God Himself is this fruit, and this is the fruit that lasts—the fruit the indwelling life of Christ is to produce in our life, for this is the image of Himself that God put into man at his creation and the very likeness that Christ came to regain for man and the Father.

We know from Genesis 1 that "like begets like"; everything reproduces "according to its own kind." There can be no crossing over from one species to another; this is a limit that God has put on all things (thereby disproving any possibility of the theory of evolution outright, by the way). So when Christ was raised from the dead and became a life-giving spirit (1 Corinthians 15:45), He was enabled to reproduce after His own kind, which is exactly what happens when one is "born again." The newborn in Christ have His indwelling life, which is love itself with all the characteristics listed in Galatians 5:22 and 23.

Our job then becomes to produce, through the life of Christ, others of His own kind, others of our own kind, brothers and sisters in the Lord, those filled with Christ, for this is the fruit that will last, which the Father seeks. We have others "in the field" to help us in our labors, of course, even the body of Christ. Some will plant, others water, and still others weed and tend to the young plants. Esoteric? Mystical? If you think so, but to me, it seems like something very tangible and marvelous!

Builders of the Kingdom

"Jesus answered, My kingdom is not of this world. If My kingdom were of this world, My servants would fight, so that I should not be delivered to the Jews; but *now* My kingdom is not from here." (Emphasis mine)

—John 18:36

"Your kingdom come, Your will be done on earth as it is in heaven."

—Matthew 6:10

"In those days John the Baptist came preaching in the wilderness of Judea, and saying, Repent, for the kingdom of heaven is at hand!"

—Matthew 3:1–2

THE FATHER, SON, and Holy Spirit created man to be their image bearer in the earth, to exercise God's rule and dominion over all creation, and to dwell (tabernacle) among mankind. What an exalted purpose and position! In other words, the Kingdom has been on the mind of God since before the foundation of the world. Satan and one third of the angels had rebelled against their Maker, and man was to defeat the enemy and return the Kingdom to the Father, that it might be "on earth as it in heaven" (Matthew 6:10).

But man chose a different path: deceived by Satan, man went his own way, deciding for himself what is good and what is evil, independent from God. All of human history has shown the tragedy of that decision. Cut off from Spirit-to-spirit communication with God, man has wandered through the world in a deformed condition, unable to even rule himself. As stated earlier, the Father, after the fall, began His search for a man who would allow Him to rule his life. No man met that condition until Jesus appeared!

And by overcoming sin, death, Satan (and self), Jesus became a "life-giving" spirit, reproducing His own kind (the purpose of rebirth in Christ). Therefore, all believers are commanded by the Lord to "follow Me," to follow His way of life—surrendered to the Father in all things—to give God full dominion and desert any trace of independence, to give His Spirit and our spirit the rule over our soul.

For that is what the Kingdom is all about, not just a glorious place to be established on the earth when Christ returns but a place in the heart and spirit *now* where all rebellion and self-reliance are gone! For such as these, the Kingdom has already come!

The book of Matthew is the book of the Kingdom, and being recorded first in the New Testament should indicate to us the central importance the coming of the Kingdom is to the Father. The ministry of John the Baptist can be summarized by the first words He spoke in the Judean desert: "Repent, for the kingdom of heaven is at hand" (Matthew 3:1). And after Jesus was baptized by John and the Holy Spirit in the wilderness, the first words of His were the same: "From that time Jesus began to preach and to say, 'Repent, for the kingdom of heaven is at hand'" (Matthew 4:17). Likewise, the disciples also did when they were sent forth.

When Jesus was being questioned by Pilate and asked if He was "the King of the Jews" (John 18:33) during His mock trial, His answer was, indeed, very interesting; He said that His kingdom was not of this world but then added a word easy to miss: *now* (v. 36), hinting, of course, that eventually the earth would be the place of His kingdom. From that day forward, Christ has been searching, even as the Father did for Him, for men and women who would submit to His rule in their lives, allowing His Kingdom to come and be established in their hearts. These are the "children of a willing heart" in one translation of Psalm 110:3, the overcomers of Revelation 2 and 3, the wise virgins of Matthew 25, the unspotted bride of Christ!

These are the builders of the Kingdom—those who are living the Kingdom now and are teaching and exhorting others to join them. Making disciples, as the Lord's command in the closing two verses of Matthew, is for this very purpose. The disciples of the true gospel have discovered the simple way of life in the Lord: just let Christ be Christ! For unless He is released and manifests, all we do is in vain. No need to form "apostolic councils" or find some way for the "five-fold" ministry to again appear (or form any other method or system). When Christ truly makes His appearance, all is well. Only if He directs us to some particular activity will it have any life in it; all other efforts are man-made and futile.

Our true identity in Christ includes being builders of His Kingdom, and we must utilize our full inheritance to succeed at this given task. O Lord, may more and more of Your people begin to see and live in Your Kingdom, for that is the only way to live holy lives and to hasten Your coming (2 Peter 3:11–12). Even so, come quickly, Lord Jesus… Maranatha!

Glory

"But we are bound to give thanks to God always for you, brethren beloved by the Lord, because God from the beginning chose you for salvation through sanctification by the Spirit and belief in the truth, to which He called you by our gospel, for the obtaining of the glory of our Lord Jesus Christ."

—2 Thessalonians 2:13–14

"The mystery which has been hidden from ages and generations, *but now has been revealed to His saints.* To them God willed to make known what are the riches of the glory of this mystery among the Gentiles: *which is Christ in you, the hope of glory.*" (Emphases mine)

—Colossians 1:26–27

"But we all, with unveiled face, beholding as in a mirror the glory of the Lord, are being transformed into the same image from glory to glory, just as by the Spirit of the Lord."

—2 Corinthians 3:18

> "For whom He foreknew, He also predestined to be conformed to the image of His Son, that He might be the firstborn among many brethren. Moreover whom He predestined, these He also called; whom He called, He also justified; and whom He justified, these *He also glorified*."
>
> —Romans 8:29–30 (emphasis mine)

SOME WORDS DEFY definition, especially those relating to God; *glory* is one of those words. Dictionary.search.yahoo.com defines it to mean great honor, praise, or distinction accorded by common consent. It is something conferring honor or renown, a highly praiseworthy asset. Sounds rather academic, anemic, and dry, doesn't it? Especially when applied to God. In the Old Testament, it was derived from a Hebrew word carrying the idea of heaviness and weight. In the New Testament, it was from a Greek word implying the idea of opinion, estimate, splendor, brightness, etc. (carm.org/dictionary).

The same source defines the phrase "glory of the Lord" as being "synonymous with splendor, honor, praise, worthiness, etc. The phrase is used to express the manifestation of God's greatness and is seen as a consuming fire, a cloud, radiance and brightness. It fills the tabernacle, can be seen, and can bring fear."

Wikipedia, the free encyclopedia, defines the closely related word, *shekinah*, as the English transliteration of a Hebrew word meaning dwelling or setting, especially relating to the divine presence of God. This was what fell in 2 Chronicles 7 when Solomon was dedicating the temple; it was so heavy that it filled the house of God to the point that the priests could not enter. This description gets us a bit closer to an understanding of what glory means when relating to God. But until we experience it ourselves, it will remain clothed in partial mystery.

When I awoke this morning, this inability to fully define the glory of God was on my mind. I quickly wrote the following, which I entitled "Pursuing the Glory":

> The glory of God to define?
> 'Tis everything He is!
>
> There is no way words can confine—
> All efforts prove remiss…
>
>
> A splendor beyond expression,
>
> Eternity falls short…
> Failure forces this confession:
> Renewed attempts abort!

And yet this is the very thing Jesus came to share with us: His glory and the glory of the Father. We are to be partakers of His divine nature, and it will be neverending, from glory to glory forever!

Certainly, in our present condition, we could not endure such things. In Exodus 40:34, God told Moses to warn the people not to gaze upon His glory at Mount Sinai, for if they did, they would surely perish. So many believers today pray for God to show them His glory but apparently not understanding what they are asking for! After Moses came down from the mountain and the presence of God, he had to veil his face from the people, for the radiance of God shining on it frightened them (Exodus 34:30–35).

That is why we will have to be changed and given a glorified body, like the Lord's; without it, we could not bear the brightness and power of His glory! For as I said in my few verses, His glory is everything He is—His wonder and His goodness in all their facets but also a consuming fire that burns up anything impure in its path! His inexorable love and unyielding justice—all this and more, so much more that we will never come to the end of it!

The glory that is waiting (and the small waves of it that we can experience now) far outweighs the hardships and tribulation we must endure on this side of the Kingdom. Paul said it like this in Romans 8:16–18: "The Spirit Himself bears witness with our spirit that we are children of God, and if children, then heirs—heirs of God and joint heirs with Christ, if indeed we suffer with Him, that we may also be glorified together. For I consider that the sufferings of this present time are not worthy to be compared with the glory which shall be revealed in us." Of all the inheritance we have in Christ, this glory is, by far, the greatest treasure and worth whatever it takes to obtain it.

Life and Death

"And out of the ground the Lord God made every tree grow that is pleasant to the sight and good for food. The tree of life was also in the midst of the garden, and the tree of the knowledge of good and evil… Then the Lord God took the man and put him in the garden of Eden to tend and keep it. And the Lord God commanded the man, saying, Of *every* tree of the garden you may freely eat: but of the tree of the knowledge of good and evil you shall not eat, for in the day that you eat of it you shall surely die." (Emphasis mine)

—Genesis 2:9, 16–17

"See I have set before you today life and good, death and evil… I call heaven and earth as witnesses today against you, that I have set before you life and death, blessing and cursing; therefore choose life, that both you and your descendants may live."

—Deuteronomy 30:15, 19

> "The thief does not come except to kill, and to steal, and to destroy. I have come that they may have life, and that they may have it more abundantly."
>
> —John 10:10

The Word of God in a nutshell concerns the matter of life and death. Even in the Garden of Eden, Adam and Eve were given that choice, for both trees were there—the tree of life and the tree of death.

They were free to eat from the tree of life (eternal life) as well as from every other tree (abundant life); the only forbidden tree was the tree of the knowledge of good and evil. If they had *first* eaten from the tree of life, the uncreated life of God would have been theirs, and history as we have come to know it would never have come to pass.

Of course, they chose pride, their own way, and the way of Satan, forfeiting the very purposes for which they had been created. Death entered and ruled, and man was cast from the garden and the intimate presence of God, the dominion intended for mankind was lost to the enemy, who became the prince of this world, a world he and fallen man have created.

The Lord God, however, is life as well as love, and His original purpose could not be permanently thwarted. After allowing man to wander for centuries and centuries in an impaired condition, never able to find lasting peace or real life, He chose for Himself a people through which to channel the life He had offered in the garden. His choice was not based on greatness, but rather lowliness, so that at long last, mankind would be humbled and realize that it is through God alone that life comes.

The small nation of Israel became God's focal point for eventually offering the tree of life to man once again. Of course, they had to be given a law by which to live—and fail at keeping—before true life could come. In Deuteronomy 30, Moses was about to be taken by God, turning over the reins of leadership to Joshua. In a very impassioned speech, he made it clear that the choice was what it had always been: life or death; life for faithfully following the commands of God or death by continuing to rebel.

Joshua, at the end of his time of leadership, at what became known as the covenant at Shechem, spoke words that were similar to those of Moses's. After entering the Promised Land, the people again had failed at trying to follow the commandments of God. In an effort to reestablish their allegiance to the Lord, Joshua laid out their choice: life or death?

In chapter 24, verses 14 and 15, he said to them: "Now therefore, fear the Lord, serve him in sincerity and in truth, and put away the gods which your fathers served on the other side of the River and in Egypt. Serve the Lord! And if it seems evil to you to serve the Lord, choose for yourselves this day whom you will serve, whether the gods which your fathers served that were on the other side of the River, or the gods of the Amorites, in whose land you dwell. *But as for me and my house, we will serve the Lord.*" (Emphasis mine)

Of course, the people all pledged to serve the Lord, but little did they know that such a pledge could never be kept. For serving the Lord includes keeping all the commandments given by God on Mt. Sinai, and such a task is impossible for carnal, unregenerated man. Fifteen hundred years under the Law (and our own lives) bear witness to this verse: "Knowing that a man is not justified by the works of the law but by faith in Jesus Christ, even we have believed in Christ Jesus, that we might be justified by faith in Christ and not by the works of the law; for by the works of the law no flesh shall be justified" (Galatians 2:16).

In the "fullness of time," the Father sent forth His only begotten Son and, by and through Him, again offered life to man. For Christ is both the tree of life and its fruit, and he who eats from that tree shall live! Did not Jesus Himself proclaim that *He* is the life, not that He was merely teaching the way to life for us to try to follow? That is where we have gone astray, reducing Christ to teachings and not the things Himself! In John 6, He says *He* is the bread of life (verses 33 and 35) and that unless we eat of that food, we have no life in us (John 6:53).

And we have already discussed how we eat of that food (Christ in us): first by repenting and believing in Christ and then by surrendering our will and life to Him, who indwells us and longs to be released and to feed us. Any other food is the nutrition of the flesh and can never sustain us or ever produce righteousness.

Jesus has come that we might have life, have it eternally and more abundantly now (John 10:10). The devil only comes to kill, steal, and destroy, and the penalty of following him and his ways is eternal separation from God in a place of torment. The pleasures of sin are for but a season, but the shared glory of God is forever. What is your choice this day? I pray with all my heart that you choose life!

Summing Up

WE HAVE COVERED much ground on our journey together. We have seen that division has been (and continues to be) Satan's main weapon in his futile effort to remain as the prince of this world and to avoid the bottomless pit and the lake of fire awaiting him. Since his defeat by Christ, the goal of our ancient foe has been to create "some other gospel," a gospel devoid of the life of Christ, a gospel of men, an emasculated and sterile gospel, powerless to produce life and set mankind free. And the flesh of man, his very soul, has aided the enemy in this endeavor. By not realizing his true makeup, spirit, soul, and body, man has unwittingly attempted to understand and carry out the works of God in his own power. Not only have those works failed, but they have also caused contention and separation in the body of Christ. Satan saw early on that he could not destroy what the Lord had accomplished on Calvary by his efforts to persecute and kill believers; in fact, those efforts only resulted in more believers! So deception, designed to bring division and weakness, became his weapon of choice, a weapon which has been very effective.

Even as early as in the days of Paul, the trouble began: Jews believed that only they or their converts to Judaism were candidates for salvation and the blessings of God. But the Holy Spirit quickly showed them the error of such thinking; not only were Gentiles to be included by the grace of God but they also did not have to first become Jews before being accepted by God.

The next places of contention, of course, were in the churches themselves. The church at Corinth was a prime example of such contention: many signs of false worship and the works of the flesh, even gross sin, surfaced at Corinth. Paul, in his first letter to the Corinthians, did all he could to point out and correct the deviations from the true gospel that were rampant in the church. How his corrections and exhortations were received and followed, we do not know for certain. His second letter seems to indicate that there had been some changes made but that "some other gospel" was definitely gaining a foothold in the church.

In our study of the seven churches of Revelation 2 and 3, we saw a pattern of what a corrupted gospel brings in its wake. Beginning with the church at Ephesus, where "first love" had been left behind and ending at the lukewarm church at Laodicea, a slow but steady spiritual decline is evident. Only the small flock at Philadelphia exhibited the fruits of the true gospel, with no intrusions of the counterfeit mentioned by Christ. When those seven churches are seen as a picture of the entire church age as well as actual, individual churches at the time of John's exile on Patmos, the footprints of "some other gospel" are difficult to miss.

And so it has been down through the ages since Christ: various aberrations of the true gospel have appeared and then vanished, only to be replaced by new ones or variations of the old ones. The Holy Spirit has brought revivals of certain truths from time to time, but even these have caused additional fractures in the body of Christ. Most believers have lost their true identity, of who they are in Christ, and have operated as spiritually destitute orphans instead of utilizing the unsearchable riches rightfully theirs as the children of God. In the process, Satan has achieved his goal: he is yet the prince of this world, and Christ has not returned.

In Part 2, we discussed the desperate need and means to recover the true gospel. That turned out to be rather simple and straightforward, for the answer is Christ Himself—Christ living in us, being released, and manifesting His Life. We must live our lives as Christ lived His: surrendering our will to Him, even as He surrendered His to the Father, releasing the Life within us to come forth with surpassing power and glory, to exchange our life for Christ's, who has imparted His own to us. Us in Christ and Christ in us, released—this alone is the true gospel.

Learning to rest in God, completely trusting His finished work, is the essential first step, ceasing from our own work the necessary prerequisite to entering that rest.

It is God within us who has done (and will do) the work; not *instead of us* but *through us*!

We were only able to make a tentative approach to accomplishing the purpose of Part 3: Living by the Indwelling Life. I personally have only been able to live in this manner from time to time, never continually, but I have also seen enough fruit produced during those times to know that this is the right path, the one leading to the tree of life and away from the tree of the knowledge of good and evil. The truth is that there is no easy one through seven steps to abide there, no simple how-to if you will. But the blessed Holy Spirit, who has been sent to see us home, will do all in His power to direct and correct us on our way! We must simply grow more intimate with Him and listen!

We have spoken of the dangers of isolation living, the Lone Ranger Christian life some have called it, isolated from living in community and as an integral and functioning part of the body of Christ. No one can spiritually survive for very long separated from the body, and detached from other parts of the body, one can do nothing of lasting value for the work of the Lord. The Lord ordained that we labor and express His life as a unified body, of which He is the head. And taking Communion, often and in the right spirit in remembrance of Him, is essential for such unity and power; the taking of the bread and the wine strengthens the spirit, and weakens the flesh.

The unity of the Spirit is a basic requirement for producing fruit that lasts, fruit that will build the Kingdom, even while on earth, and fruit that will nourish and sustain into eternity. For that is what we are to be as disciples of Christ—builders of the Kingdom, a Kingdom of believers and overcomers who will submit to the rule of the King in all things, those who will not only be citizens of the Kingdom but those who will share in the inexpressible glory of God, passing from glory to glory forever!

Afterword

It remains unclear just where we are in prophetic history. Some believe we are on the very brink of the Lord's return, no more major prophecy requiring fulfillment before His Second Coming. We are certainly in a period of spiritual decline, in great need of another great awakening. Some teach that just such a revival will take place before Christ comes again, but I do not find any scriptural evidence that this will necessarily occur.

Surely, during the time of the Tribulation, many will come to Christ such as fence sitters and those not fully committed to the Lord, and even those in deep rebellion if they belong to God. Once the writing is on the wall, so to speak, many will be moved to repent and reach out for salvation. This final in-gathering of those who are His is the very reason and purpose for such an unprecedented time of trial and suffering. But what about now? Is there still time to avert judgment by recovering and living out the true gospel?

Whether there is or not, I feel it is my duty to write this book, to speak the truth the Spirit has shown me, to give comfort and encouragement to those who hunger for more of God, to stir the complacent and lukewarm to awaken, to build the Kingdom and produce lasting fruit, to beckon the willing hearts in this, the day of His battle, to snatch a few from the fire, but first and foremost to give all the glory and honor to the One who has given His all for us!

There are many in the church world who realize how dire our spiritual situation in this country has become. The reactions to that realization have been just as plentiful: some harken back to the founding of our nation and long for a return to those principles and foundation; others lobby for more conservative political candidates, those who say they adhere to Christian values; still, others see the need for a great revival (but do little to help bring that about).

But unfortunately, most preaching and church activities continue as they always have, as though nothing is wrong, serving only to support the status quo and the building of a larger congregation. Was this not clearly foretold by Christ's assessment of the church in Laodicea: "Because you say, 'I am rich, have become wealthy, and have need of nothing'—and *do not know* that you are wretched, miserable, poor, blind, and naked—I counsel you to buy from Me gold refined in the fire; and white garments, that you may be clothed, that the shame of your nakedness may not be revealed; and anoint your eyes with eye salve, *that you may see*" (Revelation 3:17–18). (Emphases mine)

What is it about human nature that causes us to forget God so easily once the blessings for our faithfulness to

Him begin to flow? Israel was guilty of this frailty and fault many times in its history, as has been the church, and that seems to be where we are now, a time in which there is a form of godliness but very little power. As I speak to many fellow believers about the extreme spiritual urgency of our condition before the Lord, many agree but do not seem willing to do much about it. There is no sense of desperation, no prolonged period of falling on our faces in repentance and crying out to God. Instead, most efforts for change only address the symptoms, a new program or more teaching offered up, neither of which results in making any real and lasting difference.

We must come to see the very cause and core of the problem, not just deal with the peripheral effects. We have allowed ourselves to promote and follow "some other gospel," a gospel that is, in many ways, devoid of Christ! Our true and only need is Him—He who is the embodiment of all things spiritual! When He manifests Himself, all areas of our decline and apostasy will be eliminated and return us to the place He has reserved for us to be blessed: abiding in Him!

The little bracelets with the letters WWJD have become popular in recent days. What would Jesus do? That is the question. But as "spiritual" as that sounds, it is not the answer to our dilemma, for it implies that *we* must try to do whatever we think the answer to the question is; that way, we will be "like Jesus" and do the "right" thing. But that is not what Jesus meant when He said, "Follow Me," nor what Paul meant when He exhorted us in 1 Corinthians 4:16: "Therefore I urge you, imitate me." Both of them were speaking of the very pattern of their lives, how they lived from day to day: Christ surrendered to His Father in all things, and Paul submitted to the will of Christ.

(In view of that reality, WWJD would be better translated as: What *will* Jesus do? Or we can change the letters to WIJD: What *is* Jesus doing? For it is He and He alone who must do the work *through* us if we are to call any effort truly spiritual and see God's desired results.)

So how is it then that we should live in such desperate times as these? First and foremost, in prayer—in deep and persistent prayer, repenting and beseeching the Lord to extend His mercy and grace and to withhold His hand of judgment long enough for the church to be awakened (and pleading with Him to wake others up). And we must continue to live simple lives of faithfulness, resting in His faithfulness no matter what may come. And, of course, all the while we must desire, above all things, for His return! For until He comes, nothing will be made permanently right.

WDJD? What *did* Jesus do? That is a good question to ask ourselves. For remember, during His first advent, the conditions in Israel were even worse than they are in America today. Their nation was occupied and controlled by Rome; while they were free to worship their God in their own way (so long as it did not cause the empire any trouble), politically, they were powerless. So what did Jesus do? He certainly did not get involved in government, neither did He advocate rebellion or revolution. He simply went about His Father's business.

I completed my first draft of this book during Christmastime, and I recently received my monthly newsletter from World Challenge, the ministry begun by David Wilkerson and now directed by his son, Gary Wilkerson. The title of the newsletter is "Accomplishing Our Christmas Purpose." In it, Mr. Wilkerson writes: "If anyone had a right to be outraged, it was Jesus. Think of the horrific genocide that took place when He was born... Jesus grew up in a culture where there were no boys his age because they had all been slaughtered. When Christ became a man he could have said, 'Herod will pay for what he did. He killed all of my Jewish brothers, so now I'll bring him down.' Our Lord didn't do that. Instead, as a young man of thirty he set about proclaiming good news—healing the sick, performing miracles, even raising the dead. In short, he kept about His Father's business."

And that is surely what we must do, growing closer and closer to the Lord and meeting opposition and spiritual apostasy with love. For as Mr. Wilkerson also says in his Christmas newsletter, "all our power rests in His love." We must not resist the evil and spiritual malaise that surround us with knee-jerk reactions, for they only stir up more contention and rob us of His peace. We must simply let

Christ be Christ in all that we do. I wrote a short poem, which I included in the introductory portion of my first book, *From the Garden to the Kingdom*, and ending this book with the same words of wisdom seems to be a good conclusion.

The Simple Truth

The gospel is Christ plus nothing,
No additives required;
Man's traditions complicating,
For by the flesh inspired…
Jesus Himself *is* the good news,
In *Him* is everything!
It is His *person* that we choose,
He is His offering!

I pray that you take those words (and this book) to heart and truly live them. Blessings to all in the coming days!

Other Works by Rod Connell

Silly Snake Rhymes…and the Real Stuff
(Children's Book)

*From the Garden to the Kingdom: God's
Eternal Purpose, Plan, and Provision*

Pilgrimage: Finding the Way Back Home

Songs of a Son: Heart-cries Along the Way

The Calling